FALKIRK COMMUNITY TRUST

30124 03091635 9

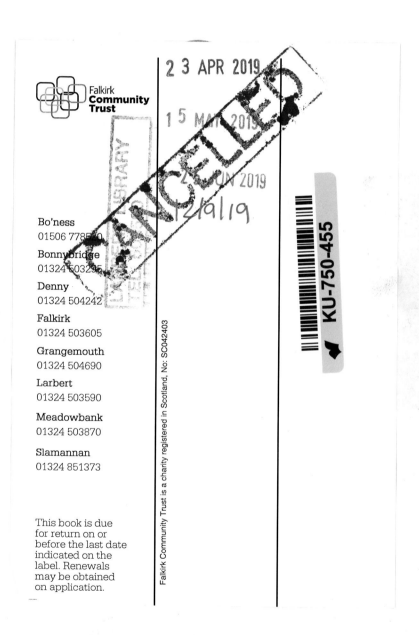

Falkirk
Community
Trust

2 3 APR 2019

1 5 MAY 2019

2019

12/9/19

CANCELLED

Bo'ness
01506 778520

Bonnybridge
01324 503235

Denny
01324 504242

Falkirk
01324 503605

Grangemouth
01324 504690

Larbert
01324 503590

Meadowbank
01324 503870

Slamannan
01324 851373

Falkirk Community Trust is a charity registered in Scotland, No: SC042403

KU-750-455

This book is due
for return on or
before the last date
indicated on the
label. Renewals
may be obtained
on application.

FALKIRK COMMUNITY
TRUST LIBRARIES

Orders: Please contact How2Become Ltd, Suite 14, 50 Churchill Square Business Centre, Kings Hill, Kent ME19 4YU.

You can order through Amazon.co.uk under ISBN 9781912370320, via the website www.How2Become.com, Gardners or Bertrams.

ISBN: 9781912370320

First published 2018

Copyright © 2018 How2Become.

All rights reserved. Apart from any permitted use under UK copyright law, no part of this publication may be reproduced or transmitted in any form or by any means, electronic or mechanical, including photocopying, recording, or any information, storage or retrieval system, without permission in writing from the publisher or under licence from the Copyright Licensing Agency Limited. Further details of such licenses (for reprographic reproduction) may be obtained from the Copyright Licensing Agency Ltd, Saffron House, 6-10 Kirby Street, London EC1N 8TS.

Typeset for How2Become Ltd by Gemma Butler.

Falkirk Community Trust	
30124 03091635 9	
Askews & Holts	
363. 2076	£13.00
LB	

Disclaimer

Every effort has been made to ensure that the information contained within this guide is accurate at the time of publication. How2Become Ltd is not responsible for anyone failing any part of any selection process as a result of the information contained within this guide. How2Become Ltd and their authors cannot accept any responsibility for any errors or omissions within this guide, however caused. No responsibility for loss or damage occasioned by any person acting, or refraining from action, as a result of the material in this publication can be accepted by How2Become Ltd.

The information within this guide does not represent the views of any third-party service or organisation.

Contents

Hello, and welcome to *Scottish Police Interview: Sample practice questions and responses*, the most comprehensive guide to the Scottish Police interview section available! In this guide, we're going to give you a detailed run through of exactly what the Scottish Police Interview involves, and how to ace it. Using FIFTY sample questions and answers, we'll provide you with a comprehensive chance to practice every single type of question that you could face in the interview.

So, without further ado, let's get started!

Police Scotland: An Introduction

Police Scotland, or The Police Service of Scotland (to go by its formal title) is a fairly new organisation, having been only formally established in 2013. Today, it is the second largest police service in the UK, with the Met Police being the biggest. At the top of the Police Scotland hierarchy is the Chief Constable, and this rank is closely followed by a Deputy Chief Constable and Assistant Chief Constables. The Police Scotland HQ is based in Fife, the same location as the Scottish Police College, where police training is held.

As you might have guessed, the work that Police Scotland do is designed to safeguard and protect the Scottish public. In order to do this, there are 13 local policing divisions in total. Each division is headed by a Local Police Commander, and contains officers including:

• First response officers;

• Community officers;

• Public protection officers;

• Intelligence officers.

Police Scotland also has a number of specialist units, such as counter-terrorism, major crime investigation, air support, and canine training. Every year, Police Scotland publishes what is known as an Annual Police Plan, to ensure that they are delivering the best possible level of service to the Scottish Public. In this plan, the service outlines their yearly aims, strategies, and priorities, for safeguarding the Scottish public.

When attending your interview, it's really important that you have some knowledge about the current state of affairs with Police Scotland. You should be able to demonstrate some organisational knowledge of Police

Scotland, and be able to show that you've researched present-day Police Scotland initiatives. The more research you can demonstrate, the better. This will show your interviewers that you have really taken the time to research the organisation, that you are interested, and that you care about the role.

Now that we've given you a brief introduction to Police Scotland, it's time to have a look at a fundamental part of the application process – the core competencies!

Police Scotland: Core Competencies

When attending any interview, one of the fundamental things that you need to consider is the core competencies of the organisation that you are applying to. This is extremely important in the police service, who have a very strict of values, ethics, and behaviour for their employees. The police play an extremely important role in society, and need to ensure that they can behave with professionalism, decency, and integrity – so that the general public can trust in them. In order to guarantee this, Police Scotland have a specific code of conduct that they expect candidates to abide by. This code emcompasses the core competencies, which are listed below:

Effective Communication

Communication is incredibly important when working in the police, and therefore it is essential that candidates can demonstrate an ability to put across their ideas in a clear and concise manner, in both written form and verbal. Working in the police will put you in contact with a wide variety of people, from different backgrounds, and therefore it's vital that you can communicate effectively. Not only will you utilise your communication skills when dealing with members of the public, but you will also need to communicate with different members of the law enforcement team, and professionals from outside of the police – such as social workers or lawyers. You may also be asked to appear in court, where you will need to communicate verbally. Alternatively, your written reports could be used in court as evidence. These are just some of the many reasons that communication is essential for police officers.

A police officer who has **good communication** can:

- Communicate effectively in writing as well as verbally;

- Identify when it is appropriate to use certain styles of communication and language;

- Adapt their communication according to the individual(s) being addressed;

- Use grammar, spelling, and punctuation effectively and correctly;

- Listen carefully when they are being spoken to, taking note of essential information;

- Influence the behaviour of others in a positive way, using good communication.

Personal Effectiveness

Personal effectiveness roughly translates to taking responsibility and ensuring that you can achieve results to the level that Police Scotland expect. It's about making sure that your own standards are up to scratch, and that you are always looking to improve and better yourself. In order to do this, you must be able to demonstrate qualities such as commitment, perseverance, and integrity, as well as a strong drive to increase the quality of your performance. Naturally, this is very important when working in the police, who demand the highest possible standards of their employees. Every single member of the police service has a responsibility to maintain an impeccable standard of work, and be willing to adapt and grow with the changing demands of the police.

A police officer who has good **personal effectiveness** can:

- Take personal responsibility for achieving results to the highest possible standard;

- Show commitment, motivation and perseverance towards police tasks;

- Understand the need for change and be willing to adapt to new methods of police practice;

- Work within an agreed timeframe, setting realistic personal objectives and goals;

- Demonstrate integrity and professionalism, in line with the police code of ethics.

Team Working

Teamwork is extremely important when working in the police. Your ability to work in synchronisation with your colleagues, to create an effective and organised policing unit, will be paramount to the success of Police Scotland. The better police staff can work together, the stronger the level of care that you can provide to the public. Policing is not a one-person job. It takes the combined efforts of the entirety of Police Scotland to fight crime successfully. As an officer, you will need to call on the help of many other specialists working within the police, and in outside agencies, so it's essential that your teamworking skills are top notch.

A police officer who has good **team working skills** can:

- Develop good professional and personal relationships with colleagues;

- Participate in group activities and team-based exercises, playing an important role in these endeavours;

- Take the views and opinions of others into account, and is prepared to discuss the views of others in a polite and amicable fashion;

- Utilise an open, honest and supportive approach when assisting other colleagues;

- Accept that not all tasks need to be completed solo, and ask for help when appropriate.

Respect for Diversity

As a police officer, it's hugely important that you have respect for diversity. You certainly cannot work within the police service without this. This essentially involves considering and showing respect for the opinions, circumstances, and feelings of colleagues and members of the public, no matter their race, religion, position, background, circumstances, status, or appearance. It is essential that you can take an unbiased and fair-minded approach to dealing with every single member of the public, and that you can understand and respect the needs of people from different backgrounds. Remember that the police are there to serve every single law-abiding citizen, and not just people from select backgrounds, and therefore it's vital that you have a good understanding of every person's needs and beliefs.

A police officer with **respect for diversity** can:

- Respect the values and feelings of people from a diverse range of backgrounds;

- Treat every single person that they meet with the utmost respect and fairness;

- Be diplomatic when dealing with all members of the public;

- Understand the need to be sensitive to differing social, cultural and racial requirements;

- Immediately challenge any inappropriate or discriminatory behaviour.

Job Knowledge

Naturally, job knowledge is another essential competency. As in any line of work, it's extremely important for police employees to have a full and capable understanding of their role, what it involves, and what their key responsibilities and duties are. Obviously, this is something that will become much more apparent when you start working for the police, but you are still expected to have a basic knowledge when applying. Prior to application, you'll need to research into topics such as your local force's priorities, what training they offer and the type of work that they do. You should expect to be asked questions based around these subjects during the interview.

A police officer with good **job knowledge** can:

• Show the assessors that they are aware of the physical and mental demands of working in the police;

• Demonstrate that they are aware of the behavioural standards of the police, and can act accordingly;

• Understand the importance of adhering to established police procedures and policies;

• Display an appreciation for all of the elements that go into working as a successful police officer, and make a sustained effort to go above and beyond expectations, whenever possible.

Personal Awareness

Personal awareness is a really important quality for a police officer to have. As officers of the law, it is vital that police employees can understand how their own behaviour has an impact on others. You need to act with empathy and diplomacy when dealing with members of the public, and with your own colleagues. The only way that you can do this is if you have a firm understanding of your own emotions. You must be able to recognise how your emotions can impact upon your performance, and how this could affect the way you deal with others. Working as a police officer is mentally taxing, as well as physically. There will be times when you aren't in the best state of mind or mood, but it is vital that you can adopt ways of dealing with this, or of recognising when you need to take yourself away from a particular situation.

A police officer with good **personal awareness** can:

- Demonstrate a good understanding of how their behaviour impacts those around them;

- Deal with sensitive situations, in an appropriate and diplomatic manner;

- Listen to the views of others, and recognise flaws in their own methods or ideas;

- Learn how to manage their own emotions, and limit disruptive thoughts or feelings, so that their performance is consistent;

- Have confidence in their own ability to perform to a high standard.

Problem Solving

Problem solving is another essential competency. Much of police work involves using common sense to make decisions and draw logical conclusions. You must be someone who can think analytically and assess situations in a calm and logical fashion. Your judgement as a police officer is extremely important, and it's imperative that you can make logical use of evidence when it presents itself.

A police officer with good **problem solving** can:

- Gather information from a wide variety of sources, to help identify potential solutions to problems;

- Work within established police procedures and systems, to find solutions to problems;

- Assess the benefits and negatives of potential decisions;

- Justify their decisions with sound reasoning and logic;

- Accept responsibility for their decisions and learn from their own mistakes.

Service Delivery

Service delivery is all about focusing on the needs of the customer – which in this case is the general public. In a nutshell, service delivery means providing the public with the best possible care and service. Essentially, you need to be able to do your job to the highest standards and remember that safeguarding the public is your number one priority. In doing this, you will need to deal with complaints, learn how to reassure distressed individuals, and develop good relationships with community members of the area in which you are policing.

A police officer with good **service delivery** can:

- Evaluate the individual needs of specific customers;

- Prioritise requests from members of the public, taking into account ongoing tasks and projects;

- Develop a good relationship with members of the community;

- Respond to customer feedback in an appropriate manner;

- Ensure that members of the public feel valued and safeguarded by the police service.

Leadership

Leadership is an important quality for any police officer to have. As a police officer, it's essential that you can act as a role model for others, and lead by example. With this in mind, police officers need to behave in an exemplary fashion. This applies both at the station, and whilst out in public. In the latter example, it's very important that the public can look to officers for reassurance and guidance on the correct way to behave. You must act in a thoughtful and fair manner and be able to think through the implications of your decisions.

A police officer with good **leadership** can:

- Act as a role model and a good example for others;

- Behave with integrity and professionalism, ensuring that all of their decisions are made with fairness in mind;

- Make big judgement calls when necessary and be prepared to take ownership for these decisions;

- Gain the trust of police colleagues, and members of the public.

Partnership Working

Partnership working is extremely important for the police service, and closely relates with teamwork. It's essential that the police service can work in tandem with partner agencies, to provide the best possible service to the public. Working in the police is all about taking a joint approach to solving problems. Whether that's with your own colleagues or with external staff, a problem shared is a problem halved. With this in mind, it's important that you are able to demonstrate a polite, open-minded and courteous approach to members of other agencies.

A police officer with good **partnership-working** skills can:

- Establish good relationships with staff from partner agencies;

- Respect and adhere to the organisational policies and expectations of partner agencies, when working with them;

- Utilise good teamworking skills to work in conjunction with staff from other agencies;

- Act as an exemplary representative of the police service, when working with partner agencies;

- Consider the views and opinions of others, when making decisions.

Why Are the Competencies So Important?

At this point, you might be thinking that these competencies aren't important for you yet, given that you are only applying for the job. Well, think again, because they are extremely important! The core competencies are an essential part of the job application process, and your chances of success very much rest on how well you understand them, and how well you can demonstrate them. Throughout the application process, the police service will be constantly testing you, looking for you to demonstrate the core competencies. The interview questions will be heavily focused around the competencies, and each one will require you to demonstrate a different competency. So, you need to revise each one extremely carefully. Not only that, but you need to try and think of past examples/times when you have demonstrated this competency, and used it to resolve an issue.

Competency-Based Questions

Competency-based questions are becoming more and more common in job interviews, and therefore it's essential that you are prepared for how to answer them. A competency-based question is one which focuses on a specific competency, and how you've used the competency in the past. For example, you might be asked:

Give us an example of a time when you have demonstrated good team working skills.

Here, the question takes a very direct approach, directly referencing the competency. However, not all of the questions will be this obvious. You might be asked something like:

Do you see yourself as someone who works well with others? What attributes do you have that make you a good colleague?

This question is asking roughly the same thing, but the question is a bit more subtle, and requires you to think a bit harder about what is being asked. You still need to demonstrate a past example of when you've used that behaviour, and a knowledge of how it applies to the job role.

When answering competency-based questions, it's really important that you do not fall into the trap of providing a 'generic' response that details what you 'would do' if the situation arose, unless of course you have not been in this type of situation before. Instead, you need to say what you DID do.

When responding to situational questions, try to structure your responses in a logical and concise manner. The way to achieve this is to use the 'STAR' method of interview question response construction:

Situation. Start off your response to the interview question by explaining what the 'situation' was and who was involved.

Task. Once you have detailed the situation, explain what the 'task' was, or what needed to be done.

Action. Now explain what 'action' you took, and what action others took. Also explain why you took this particular course of action.

Result. Explain to the panel what you would do differently if the same situation arose again. It is good to be reflective at the end of your responses. This demonstrates a level of maturity and it will also show the panel that you are willing to learn from every experience.

Finally, explain what the outcome or result was following your actions and those of others. Try to demonstrate in your response that the result was positive because of the action you took.

The majority of the questions will require you to focus on just one or two competencies. As long as you fully demonstrate the competencies that are being asked for in the question, then you will score good marks. You shouldn't try to force extra competencies into your answers. However, if it can be done naturally, then it's always a good idea to demonstrate these. For example, if you are answering a question about leadership, then it's completely normal for other competencies to come up too when recounting your behaviour.

The Interview Process

Police Scotland assesses candidates in a slightly different format to other UK police forces. You will face two interviews during the selection process, each of which will test you on different elements.

Initial Interview

The first interview that you take, will be done before the assessment centre. Provided you pass the standard entrance test and an initial fitness assessment, you'll be invited to interview with your local recruitment team. During the first interview, you will be quizzed on the following competencies:

- Effective communication

- Personal effectiveness

- Team work

- Respect for diversity

- Personal awareness

- Service delivery

- Job knowledge

Along with this, you may also be asked some ethics based questions, and questions based on the Police Scotland standards of professional behaviour. These questions focus around the expectations of police officers, and your motivations for applying to the police. We highly recommend that you study the Police Scotland standards of professional behaviour, and the code of ethics. We have listed both of these below:

Police Scotland Standards of Professional Behaviour

Authority, respect and courtesy

It's integral for police officers to act with self-control and tolerance, and they must be able to treat every person that they meet with kindness and courtesy.

Equality and diversity

Police officers must respect fairness and impartiality. They should never discriminate, and must only use force when necessary and proportionate.

Duties and responsibilities

In order for police officers to perform to the best of their ability, they must perform diligently in every single task that they are given.

Honesty and integrity

Police officers must act with honesty and integrity at all times, and must never abuse their position, or place themselves in a situation where their reputation might be compromised.

Orders and instructions

Police officers must recognise that they are duty bound to only give and adhere to lawful orders and instructions, and must not participate in any behaviour which could be deemed contrary to this.

Confidentiality

In order for police officers to gain the trust and respect of the general public, they must treat information with respect, and only disclose said information in a correct and lawful manner, when appropriate.

Fitness for duty

It's extremely important that officers can monitor their own performance, to ensure that they are up to the task of carrying out their responsibilities.

Discreditable conduct

Police officers must never behave in a way which damages or discredits the reputation of Police Scotland, or undermines public confidence in the police.

Challenging and reporting improper conduct

It's essential that police officers are able to take action and challenge any conduct which falls below the standards of professional behaviour for police officers.

Police Scotland Code of Ethics

Respect

Respect is a core part of working for the police. It means taking pride in your team, and showing respect for every single person, regardless of their background, gender or culture. Police officers must be able to understand the importance of upholding the law and contributing to the professional reputation of Police Scotland.

Regardless of whom you are dealing with, whether it is an innocent person or a detained individual, you must treat them in a dignified, polite and respectful manner.

Fairness

Police officers must be able to face every challenge that they meet whilst working for Police Scotland, with courage, tolerance and composure. It's essential that all employees of Police Scotland are able promote positivity and unity within the community.

In the interests of fairness, police officers must be able to take an open-minded approach to all community and social issues, and carry out every single one of their duties in an impartial and non-discriminatory manner.

Human Rights

Understanding human rights is really important for police officers. It's integral to ensure that your actions as an officer are done in a way which shows respect for human rights, and does not breach this protocol.

All employees of Police Scotland must understand the appropriate use of force, and not utilise this in circumstances where it would not be deemed appropriate, or legitimate. Prior to making any decision which requires force, officers must be able to clearly think through their actions and whether they are necessary.

Furthermore, it's essential that officers understand that people have an equal right to liberty and security, and therefore do not encourage or allow any form of torture or degradation to any other person, whether that be a member of the public or a detainee.

Finally, it's essential that police officers understand the principle of 'innocent until proven guilty'.

Integrity

Police officers must be able to recognise that their role, as an employee of Police Scotland, requires them to act with integrity at all times. It's imperative that police officers can behave in a manner that is reflective of the values of Police Scotland, and that they can take responsibility for their own behaviour.

In order to act as a role model, it's imperative that Police Scotland employees can put community service above their own personal goals, and do not participate in any behaviour that could be seen as compromising their impartiality – for example accepting gifts from members of the public, or favouring certain groups over others.

All employees of Police Scotland are expected to challenge any behaviour that they believe falls below the standards of the organisation.

Assessment Centre Interview

During the assessment centre, you will be required to take a second interview. Your score for this interview will be combined with your test results. The second interview will test you on the following areas:

- Effective communication

- Personal effectiveness

- Job knowledge

- Personal awareness

- Leadership

- Partnership working

Motivational Questions

Although both interviews will be heavily competency based, you should also expect that you'll encounter some 'motivational' questions at some point during the selection process. This could take place during the application form, and you might also be asked some during the interview too. Motivational questions are essentially questions which focus around your reasons for joining the police, and aim to establish that your values are in line with Police Scotland.

When answering the interview questions, you can expect that some of the questions will incorporate multiple elements. For example, when answering a competency based question, you might find that you are also giving the police a good demonstration of your ethics – and vice versa! This is a really good thing, as it shows that you can display multiple elements of what the police are looking for in just one situation.

In this guide, we've provided you with 25 competency based questions, and 25 motivational questions too. Along with this, we have also made a concerted attempt to test you on every single competency. You might notice, for example, that 'problem solving' is not on the list for the interview competency questions. Whilst this is true, it's still a good idea to make sure that you fully understand this competency, and why it's important. Therefore, we've included this in our question list, as it certainly doesn't hurt to show that you have this competency.

Now that we have looked into how to prepare for the interview, it is time to provide you with a number of sample questions and answers. Please note that the questions provided here are for practice purposes only and are not to be relied upon to be the exact questions that you will be asked during your final interview.

Before you move onto the next section, quickly take a look at each of the competencies we have mentioned. On a separate piece of paper, write down examples from the past of where you have demonstrated each competency. This will prepare you for the next part of the book!

Disclaimer: Please note, these questions are for example purposes only, and do not reflect the exact questions that you will be asked at the assessment centre. Likewise, the sample responses are for demonstrative purposes only and are not to be copied or to be taken as a 'perfect' answer. You must use your own experiences and ensure your answers are true to you when coming up with your own answers for the interview questions.

Competency-Based Questions

In this section of the book, we are going to provide you with some sample questions, from the competency section of the interview. We have given you 25 questions in total, to ensure that you are fully prepared for what you will face. After every question, we'll also provide you with an in-depth answer, so that you can see how your response matches up against ours! Use the answer boxes after each question to fill in your own response.

For the first question, we have given you a detailed explanation on how to answer.

Q1. Tell me about a time when you acted on your own initiative to solve a problem.

How to Answer

As you can see, the question is asking you to demonstrate when you've shown initiative. Take a look at the competencies again, which we've listed below:

- Communication;
- Personal Effectiveness;
- Team Working;
- Respect for Diversity;
- Job Knowledge;
- Personal Awareness;
- Problem Solving;
- Service Delivery;
- Leadership;
- Partnership Working.

You can see that 'taking initiative' is not a listed competency, so what you need to do now is think about which of the competencies best illustrates 'taking initiative'. In a way, all of the competencies require this, but some more than others. So, you need to give an example of where you have taken initiative, whilst using one of the above competencies. You could give an example of when you have taken initiative, whilst also demonstrating great **leadership skills**. Essentially, if the question doesn't directly ask you for a competency, then you need to find a relatable competency to the behaviour mentioned, and then link the two together.

Take a look at our sample response below for an idea of how to do this.

Sample Response

I am currently working as a sales assistant for a well-known retailer. More recently I achieved a temporary promotion and was required to manage the shop one busy Saturday afternoon.

At approximately 2pm, a customer entered the shop and approached the desk. He began complaining to a member of staff (Julie) about a coat he had purchased from our company the week before. As Julie listened to his complaint he started to get quite irate and began to raise his voice. I could see Julie becoming upset. The gentlemen then started to be verbally abusive towards her. At that point I stepped in, and calmly intervened.

First, I introduced myself as the sales assistant and informed the gentleman that I would be dealing with his complaint from here on in. I then went on to tell him that I would do all I could to resolve his complaint, but that I would not tolerate any form of aggressive, con- frontational or abusive language.

I also warned him that any further use of such communication would be reported to the police, in line with company policy. This immediately had the effect of calming down the customer, as he realised that he had already crossed the line with his comments to the other member of staff. He immediately apologised to Julie.

I then asked the customer to explain exactly what had happened and reassured him that I would resolve the issue. Whilst he explained his complaint I maintained an open and relaxed body position in order to diffuse any potential conflict and utilised effective listening skills.

The complaint in question was that the coat the man had purchased had ripped, after only one day of wearing it. Furthermore, it had ripped whilst he was out, leaving him to walk around for the day in the cold. This was the reason that he was so angry. After listening carefully to his complaint I then explained how I would resolve it for him. I fetched the manager and suggested that, in line with company policy, the customer should receive a replacement coat, and a full refund for his trouble. My manager agreed with me, and we returned to the man with our intended solution.

Once he had heard our solution, the customer was very pleased, and again apologised sincerely to Julie. I feel that throughout the situation, I maintained a resilient and professional stance, yet still managed to resolve the customer's complaint to their satisfaction.

In this answer, we've focused primarily on **communication** and **service delivery**, whilst still showing the interviewer about how we took initiative for dealing with the issue – 'At that point I stepped in, and calmly intervened.'

Now, have a go at the following questions for yourself. Some will be in the same style as the above, in which case we will give you some examples of how to link this with relevant competencies, and others will be more direct and question you on the competency itself.

Q2. Can you provide an example of when you have provided excellent service to an individual or group?

How to Answer

This question is clearly testing the core competency of **service delivery**. So, in your response, you need to cover as many possible areas of good customer service as you can. Think about a time when you've dealt directly with a customer, and the things you did to resolve their issue. What type of things did you say to them to make them feel reassured? What factors did you need to consider when making decisions? Also note that this question asks for an example of 'excellent service', so make sure that you give an example of when your behaviour was really outstanding. When answering this question, think about the following:

- What was the service that was being delivered? How would it benefit the customer?

- What did you consider when dealing with the individual or group?

- Were there any special requirements you needed to take into consideration?

- What was the final outcome? Did your behaviour resolve the issue?

Write your answer in the textbox below, and then compare it to our response!

Sample Response

"Whilst working as a shop assistant in my current role, a member of the public came in to complain about a pair of football shoes that he had bought for his son's birthday. When his son came to open the present on the morning of his birthday, he noticed that one of the football boots was a larger size than the other. He was supposed to be playing football with his friends that morning and wanted to wear his new boots. However, due to the shop's mistake, this was not possible.

Naturally, the boy was very upset. I remained calm throughout and listened to the gentleman very carefully, showing complete empathy for his son's situation. This immediately defused any potential confrontation. I then told him how sorry I was for the mistake that had happened, and that I would feel exactly the same if it was my own son who it had happened to. I made the executive decision that I would refund the money in full and give his son a new pair of football boots for the same value as the previous pair. The man was delighted with my offer. Not only that, I then offered to give the man a further discount of 10% on any future purchase, due to the added inconvenience that was caused by him having to return to the shop to sort out the problem.

In order to achieve a successful outcome, I used exceptional communication skills and remained calm throughout. The potential for losing a customer was averted by my actions and I feel sure the man would return to our shop again in the future. I am a strong believer in delivering high quality customer service and can be relied upon to be a positive role model for Police Scotland if I am to be successful."

Q3. Tell me about a time when you have taken it upon yourself to learn a new skill or develop an existing one.

How to Answer

This question is testing you on the core competencies of **personal effectiveness** and **job knowledge**. Your personal effectiveness as a police officer is directly affected by how well you can learn, improve and adapt. Remember that police officers should always be striving for improvement. In terms of job knowledge, it's also extremely important that you can stay up to date with the requirements for your role, and skills that you need to learn or improve upon. When answering this question, think about the following:

• What was the skill that you learned or developed?

• What prompted this development? Did you notice this yourself?

• How did you go about learning or developing this skill?

• How has this skill helped you since then?

Write your answer in the textbox below, and then compare it to our response!

Sample Response

"Although I am in my late thirties I had always wanted to learn to play the guitar. It is something that I have wanted to do for many years, but have never had the time to learn, until recently. One day I was watching a band play with my wife at my local pub and decided there and then that I would make it my mission to learn to play competently. The following day I went onto the Internet and searched for a good guitar tutor in my local area. Luckily, I managed to find one within my town who had a very good reputation for teaching. I immediately booked a block of lessons and started my first one within a week.

My development in the use of playing the guitar progressed rapidly and I soon achieved grade 1 standard. Every night of the week I would dedicate at least 30 minutes of time to my learning, in addition to my one-hour weekly lesson. I soon found that I was progressing through the grades quickly, which was due to my level of learning commitment and a desire to become competent in playing the instrument.

I recently achieved level 4 and I am now working to level 5 standard. I am also now playing in a local band and the opportunities for me, both musically and socially, have increased tenfold since learning to play. In addition to this, learning to play the guitar has improved my concentration levels and my patience.

Shortly after achieving my level 4 results, I decided to put my guitar skills to good use. With the help of some friends of mine, I thought it would be a fantastic idea to give something back to the community. I set about organising a set of charity beginner guitar classes, which I and my friends would teach. Initially there was some concern over whether we were experienced enough to do so, but I made the executive decision that we should target our classes at level 2 and below. This would provide us with enough of a gap in skill that our expertise would be valuable. The classes in question were a tremendous success, and we made a significant amount of money for charity.

We donated this to a child protection agency. It felt great to give back to the community, and benefit the welfare of the younger generation, which both are hugely important to me."

Q4. Tell me about a time when you noticed a member of your team behaving in an unacceptable manner.

How to Answer

This question is essentially asking you to confirm that you have what it takes to challenge poor behaviour. Notice that the question doesn't ask you to demonstrate that you challenged this behaviour, but of course it would reflect very poorly on you if you didn't, and therefore you need to show that you did.

The competency that you use here will very much depend on the situation, but a good example would be **respect for diversity**. You might have noticed someone behaving unacceptably towards another colleague, or even a member of the public. This question is your chance to demonstrate that you will stand up for what is right, and take action, when required. When answering this question, think about the following:

- What was the situation?
- How was the behaviour inconsistent with the organisation's values?
- Why were the colleagues behaving in that way?
- What did you say or do when you noticed this behaviour?
- What difficulties did you face?
- What was the result?

Write your answer in the textbox below, and then compare it to our response!

Sample Response

"Whilst working as a sales person for my previous employer, I was serving a lady who was from an ethnic minority background. I was helping her to choose a gift for her son's 7th birthday when a group of four youths entered the shop and began looking around at the goods we had for sale. They began to make racist jokes and comments to the lady. I was naturally offended by the comments and was concerned for the lady to whom these comments were directed. Any form of bullying and harassment is not welcome in any situation and I was determined to stop it immediately and protect the lady from any more harm.

The lady was clearly upset by their actions and I too found them both offensive and insensitive. I decided to take immediate action and stood between the lady and the youths to try to protect her from any more verbal abuse or comments. I told them in a calm manner that their comments were not welcome and would not be tolerated. I then called over my manager for assistance and asked him to call the police before asking the four youths to leave the shop. I wanted to diffuse the situation as soon as possible, being constantly aware of the lady's feelings. I was confident that the shop's CCTV cameras would have picked up the four offending youths and that the police would be able to deal with the situation. After the youths had left the shop I sat the lady down and made her a cup of tea whilst we waited for the police to arrive. I did everything that I could to support and comfort the lady and told her that I would be prepared to act as a witness to the racial bullying and harassment that I had just witnessed.

I believe the people acted as they did because of a lack of understanding, education and awareness. Unless people are educated and understand why these comments are not acceptable, then they are not open to change. They behave in this manner because they are unaware of how dangerous their comments and actions are. They believe it is socially acceptable to act this way, when it certainly isn't.

I also feel strongly that if I had not acted and challenged the behaviour the consequences would be numerous. To begin with I would have been condoning this type of behaviour and missing an opportunity to let the offenders know that their actions are wrong (educating them). I would have also been letting the lady down, which would have in turn made her feel frightened, hurt and unsupported. We all have the opportunity to help stop discriminatory behaviour, and providing we ourselves are not in any physical danger, then we should take positive action to stop it."

Q5. Can you provide an example of when you have planned or organised an event?

How to Answer

You'll notice that planning and organising are not a listed core competency. However, **problem solving** and **service delivery** are, so this is a great chance to demonstrate these competencies. Planning or organising an event will inevitably bring a great deal of challenges and problems for you to overcome. You need to show how you overcame these, and that you managed to do so whilst still delivering a great level of service to your customers. When answering this question, think about the following:

- What was the event? What challenges did you face initially?
- What did you consider during the planning or organising stage?
- What did you do to make sure the event went according to plan?
- What was the end result?
- How did you feel about planning and organising it in this way?

Write your answer in the textbox below, and then compare it to our response!

Sample Response

"A couple of months ago I decided to raise some money for a local children's charity. I read an article in my newspaper which detailed how the charity were looking to raise money in order to purchase some much-needed items of equipment that would help to improve disabled children's lives.

I immediately set about thinking of different ways to help. I thought about the problem in depth and came up with a list of ways in which this could be potentially be done, and the advantages and disadvantages of each method. Eventually, I narrowed the list down, and decided that a car wash event would be an ideal way to raise some money for them fast.

I sat down and created an action plan that detailed what I was going to do and by when. The plan included things such as where I would hold the event, what day the event would take place, who I would recruit to help me out, sponsors, equipment needed and public liability insurance etc. I soon realised there was a lot of work required to pull off the event, so I set myself strict deadlines to meet.

I prioritised the tasks in a logical manner and soon found a venue and date for the event to take place. I contacted my local supermarket and they agreed to help me out by providing the venue, and a date for the event to take place, which was a Saturday, their busiest day, and also public liability insurance for the event. Once I had the venue and date arranged I then needed to recruit helpers for the day. I wrote to all of my neighbours and posted messages on Facebook encouraging people to volunteer and help out – I was soon inundated with volunteers. In addition to this I wrote to the local media to seek their help in promoting the charity event.

The next stage of the planning process was to hold a meeting with the volunteers so that I could brief them on my plan for the day and explain how the event would run. This was also a good time for me to allocate tasks to different members of the team based on their strengths.

The event took place on the intended date and it was a thorough success. To my surprise, we managed to raise over £2,000 for the local charity. I believe the success of the event was entirely down to how I planned it from the get go."

Q6. Give me an example of a time when you have had to work under pressure.

How to Answer

Working for the police is a highly-pressured role, and there are times when you will find yourself up against it. You'll be faced with difficult situations, and will need to make fast decisions based on limited information. Therefore, it's important for Police Scotland to establish that you are someone who can handle this. They need candidates who are resilient and determined, whilst still being able to remain calm and logical in difficult situations. Your decision making and ability to perform under pressure will be crucial to your success in this role. When answering this question, try and think about the following:

- What was the situation? What would the consequences have been if you did not succeed?

- How did you go about tackling the task? Did you use any self-management strategies?

- How did you feel whilst completing the task?

- What was the end result? Did you complete the task?

Write your answer in the textbox below, and then compare it to our response!

Sample Response

"Previously, I worked as a teacher. Whilst training for this role, I was under constant pressure with deadlines. Combined with lesson planning, placements and teaching, this made for perhaps one of the most difficult but rewarding years of my life.

I would say that the climax of this came during late April, when I had two course-changing assignments due in, whilst at the same time was teaching 4 days a week in placement schools. This was incredibly stressful, but I'm extremely proud of how I managed my time and work under such pressurised circumstances.

Knowing how difficult the month would be, I sat down at the start of the month and planned out exactly how and when I would go about taking key tasks, managing my essays and planning/teaching lessons at the same time. While I understood that school placements would take up the majority of my time, I was absolutely determined to achieve top marks in my assessments. At the same time however, I acknowledged that my performance in both areas would suffer if I did not make time for myself – so it was important to find the right balance.

With careful planning and organisation, creating a detailed timetable that listed when and where each task would be carried out (and sticking to it!) I managed to balance out the month and received top marks in my essays, all the while teaching great lessons in my placement schools.

The biggest thing I have learned from this experience is that you can't always plan to perfection. There are always unexpected issues that can come up. Luckily, I am prepared to take on any challenge, regardless of how unexpected it is."

Q7. Can you provide an example of when you have prioritised a task, in order to maximise efficiency?

How to Answer

This is an interesting question, and in some ways it's a trick question too. You can see that the question is asking you about efficiency. However, it's also indirectly asking you to show that you can work in an efficient manner, without sacrificing the quality of the work or your performance. This comes down to **personal effectiveness** and **problem solving**. In your response, you will need to show that you recognised the gravity of the situation, and took the initiative to prioritise and complete the task. When answering this question, think about the following:

- What was the task? How did you approach it?

- Were there any rules or instructions that you had to follow?

- What did you do to complete the task?

- What was the result?

- How did you feel about completing the task in this way?

Write your answer in the textbox below, and then compare it to our response!

Sample Response

"In my current job as a car mechanic for a well-known company, I was presented with a difficult and pressurised situation that required me to work unsupervised in a fast, methodical and safe manner. A member of the team had made a mistake and had fitted a number of wrong components to a car. The car in question was due to be picked up at 2pm and the customer had stated how important it was that his car was ready on time because he had an important meeting to attend. We only had two hours in which to resolve the issue and I volunteered to be the one who would carry out the work on the car.

The problem was that we had three other customers in the workshop waiting for their cars too, so I was the only person who could be spared at that particular time. I started out by looking at the task in a methodical manner and put a plan together that would enable me to complete each task within a set timeframe. I then set about my work solidly for the next two hours, making sure that I meticulously carried out each task in line with our operating procedures and my training. I completed the task just before 2pm. I managed to achieve everything that I set out to achieve, whilst following strict safety procedures and regulations.

I understand that the role of a police officer will require me to work under extreme pressure at times and I believe I have the experience to achieve this. I am very meticulous in my work and always ensure that I take personal responsibility to keep up-to-date with procedures and policies in my current job."

Q8. Tell me about a time when you sought to improve the way that you do things, following feedback from someone else.

How to Answer

Working as a police officer means that you need to be constantly improving the way that you work. This relates to your **personal awareness**, and your **communication.** When answering this question, you need to demonstrate that a) you improved your methods, and b) that this had positive results on the way that you work. The ability to listen and take on board feedback is a key part of communication, and it's essential that you are someone who can listen to the views of others, and show an appreciation for what they are saying – especially if that person is either a customer or a senior member of the police. When answering this question, think about the following:

- What was the improvement that you made?

- What prompted this change?

- What did you personally do to ensure that the change was successful?

- What was the result?

Write your answer in the textbox below, and then compare it to our response!

Sample Response

"I currently work as a telecommunications engineer and I have been doing this job for nine years now. I am very well qualified, and can carry out the tasks that form part of my job description both professionally and competently. However, with the introduction of wireless telecommunications I started to feel a little bit out of my depth. Wireless telecommunications provide telephone, Internet, data, and other services to customers through the transmission of signals over networks of radio towers. The signals are transmitted through an antenna directly to customers, who use devices such as mobile phones and mobile computers to receive, interpret, and send information. I knew very little about this section of the industry and decided to ask my line manager for an appraisal. During the appraisal I raised my concerns about my lack of knowledge in this area and she agreed to my request for continuing professional training in this important area.

As part of my role, I often have to communicate directly with customers, dealing with their issues and queries. Given that I was learning a variety of new things, I felt that it was my responsibility to make sure that I was fully equipped to help all of our customers out to the best of my ability. Along with the new training that I would be provided with, I also sought out advice from my line manager on the best way to link my new skills with great customer service. Together, we ran through a plan of action that would allow me to do so.

I was soon booked on a training course which was modular in nature and took seven weeks to complete. During the training I personally ensured that I studied hard, followed the curriculum and checked with the course tutor periodically to assess my performance and act on any feedback they offered.

At the end of the training I received a distinction for my efforts. I now felt more comfortable in my role at work and I also started to apply for different positions within the company that involved wireless technology. For the last six months I have been working in the wireless telecommunications research department for my company and have excelled in this new area of expertise."

Q9. Can you give me an example of when you have worked as part of a team to successfully resolve an issue?

How to Answer

This is probably the easiest question to answer so far! It's very clear here about exactly what the question is asking for – it wants you to demonstrate great **teamwork**! Think about all of the aspects that go into working as part of a team, and how you demonstrated your ability to work with others. Make sure you explain exactly what the issue was, how the group overcame it, and what your role was. When answering this question, think about the following:

- What was the issue that the team faced? Did you have a deadline in which to resolve it?

- How did the team react in the face of adversity?

- What did you say or do to help encourage your teammates?

- What was your role in the project? How did you benefit the effort?

- What was the end result?

Write your answer in the textbox below, and then compare it to our response!

Sample Response

"When I was working in my previous position as an administrator, I was required to work in teams on a daily basis. Often, I was positioned as the leader of these teams. On one occasion that I can remember, our task was to organise a company-wide event. This would involve hiring out independent entertainment workers, food suppliers, health and safety specialists and other essential staff. I was one of three sub-leaders of the team and had around 30 people under my command.

My main priority was finding the relevant healthy and safety staff. I did this because health and safety at such an event should be a top priority. It is the responsibility of the company to ensure that they have met recognised safety standards, and to maintain the wellbeing of all attendees at their event. Also, in the event of an injury, a failure to implement health and safety procedures could seriously damage the business. I made contact with the paramedical department of the local hospital, and requested if they could free up several members of staff and at least two vehicles, for the day of the event. I then liaised with both of the other team leaders, to ensure that I had all of the details of exactly what they were planning. I paid particular attention to the entertainments organiser. Between us, we worked out exactly which health and safety procedures would need to be put in place to accommodate the activities being arranged.

Following this meeting, I instructed the team under my control to make contact with the local fire service, and the local police service, and request for staff members from each sector to be available on the day of the event. We successfully negotiated a time and fee.

The event was a tremendous success and there were no serious injuries to report. At the end of the event, I was congratulated by my boss on my efforts in securing the participation of these crucial safety management services."

Q10. Can you give me an example of a time when you have used good communication to solve a difficult problem?

How to Answer

Again, this is a very simple question, that wants you to demonstrate your proficiency with **communication**. Like the previous question, this is asking how you've used communication to resolve a problem. You'll notice that a lot of these questions follow the trend of asking you how you've solved a problem. The interviewers don't just want to see that you can demonstrate the competency, but they want to see how you can use it in a positive and effective manner – to help customers. When answering this question, think about the following:

- What was the issue?

- Who did you need to communicate with, in order to resolve it?

- How did good communication help to solve the problem?

- What steps did you take, that resulted in a positive outcome?

Write your answer in the textbox below, and then compare it to our response!

Sample Response

"For the majority of the modules on my degree, I was required to perform a group presentation. This presentation formed a part of the final mark for that module. In one particular module, I was placed in a presentation group with 3 foreign students who struggled with the English language. When you are presenting, you are awarded marks for communication. Therefore, a failure to speak in clear sentences could have resulted in us being penalised. I realised that, in order for us to succeed, I would have to take leadership of the group. I arranged an initial meeting in order to establish what roles everyone would have in the presentation, and to establish what their strengths and weaknesses were.

I felt that it was important for every single member of the group to demonstrate that they could communicate effectively, and speak in the presentation. Therefore, I wrote out some very basic material for them to read, so everyone would gain a communication mark. When it came to the presentation, I took on the majority of the speaking, but made sure that everyone else had a turn.

Without my input, I feel that the members of the team would have struggled to communicate or even organise a meeting. I was responsible for organising which part of the presentation each member would be responsible for, as well as creating PowerPoint slides and written content. We ultimately received a 2:1 for the presentation, and were awarded a 9/10 for communication."

Q11. Can you give me an example of a time when you have demonstrated your leadership qualities?

How to Answer

This question is asking you to demonstrate your **leadership** skills. As you will know, leadership is a very important quality for any police officer to have. Leadership is about making important decisions, acting as an example to others, and gaining the trust of your colleagues and customers – through professional and honest behaviour. Try to give the assessors an account that demonstrates a) that your colleagues had trust in you to make a decision b) that your decision was the right one, and had positive implications. When answering this question, think about the following:

- What was the situation, and why did it require strong leadership skills?

- If you had make key decisions, what were they, and how did you come to these decisions?

- What was the (positive) outcome of your decision?

- What did you learn from the experience?

Write your answer in the textbox below, and then compare it to our response!

Sample Response

'During my time as an administrator, I was often required to make difficult decisions. One such occasion that I can remember was when a member of my team turned up to work in an inebriated state. The individual in question had undergone severe personal trauma. While he had been offered time off to deal with this, he had refused.

Some of the other members of the management team felt that the best course of action was to send him home and release him from the company. They were uncomfortable with his behaviour and believed that, because he refused to take time off, attending the office in this state was extremely unprofessional. They could not seem to agree on what should be done. As a member of the management team, I decided to take leadership of the situation. I informed the other staff members of this, and promised them that I would make a fair and reasonable decision.

My first decision was what to do with the employee on an immediate basis. While I would certainly be sending him home, I decided that my options were a) to call the police, b) to assign someone from the office to take him home, or c) to use a contact number for someone to collect him and take him home. I decided upon option C. While there were a number of willing volunteers, I did not want to further damage the day's work. A relative of the employee arrived swiftly and took him home in her car.

My second decision was whether the employee should be sacked. I weighed up all of the options before making this decision. If we fired him, we would be showing a lack of sensitivity and understanding as a company. If we did not fire him, we might be setting a bad example. I ultimately decided that I was prepared to give him one final chance, since this was the first time it had happened. The individual in question was a very capable employee and losing him would only damage the business.

I called the employee the next morning, and spoke to him about the situation. I informed him in a sensitive manner that if he wished to keep his job, then he a) needed to take some time off to deal with his issue, and b) needed to use this time to seek therapy or guidance. I reassured him that the company would support him through this difficult period in his life.

The end result of this situation was that the employee took a two-week break, and came back feeling better. He is still at the company, and has now risen to a management position. I believe that by taking leadership of the situation, I ultimately aided the company long term."

Q12. Can you give me an example of when you have worked with individuals from other agencies to resolve a problem?

How to Answer

This directly relates to the core competency of **partnership working.** This is an extremely important quality for police officers to have, as Police Scotland works with a variety of outside agencies in order to achieve their goals. It's imperative that you can coordinate effectively with employees from these agencies, and in a polite and amicable manner, whilst representing the interests of Police Scotland. When answering this question, think about the following:

- What was the problem that needed to be resolved?

- How did you decide which individuals/agencies, to involve? Why did you choose them?

- How did you go about implementing a plan of action to resolve the issue?

- What steps did you personally take, to ensure the matter was solved?

- What was the final outcome?

Write your answer in the textbox below, and then compare it to our response!

Sample Response

"Whilst working as an administrator at my previous company, I was part of the team responsible for managing external projects. One of our clients came to us, asking for us to organise an event. The company in question was one of the top providers of business software in the UK, and therefore client events were extremely important for pushing their products and increasing revenue. The company informed us that unfortunately, from 2013 till 2014, there had been a marked drop in the attendance of their events. I was tasked with fixing this, for the next event.

When it came to planning the 2015 event, I knew that it was extremely important to boost attendances again. With the help of my team, we interviewed the sales representatives at the company. They felt that there a lack of direct advertising and marketing for the events, and that if we wanted to boost attendance, we needed to use social media to make people more aware that the events were taking place.

I personally wrote up a questionnaire, which was dispatched to past attendees of our events, requesting feedback on how the events could be improved. Based on this feedback, I drew up an entirely new network and marketing plan for the events. This included improving the social media coverage of the event and hiring social media experts to increase its exposure.

The end result of this was that, for our client's 2015 events, they broke their record for attendances. Their client base responded extremely well to the improved social media coverage, and this resulted in a huge increase in revenue for the year. Feedback reports said that the client base was very happy with the improved networking strategy, and that they would be highly likely to recommend such events to their friends and family."

Q13. Can you give me an example of a time when you have improved the way you work, using the feedback of others?

How to Answer

This question wants you to demonstrate that you have the ability to listen to feedback and take it on board, and then use it in a constructive manner. The most relevant competency here would be **personal awareness**. Personal awareness means accepting constructive criticism from others, recognising that everyone makes mistakes, and learning from your own errors. It's very important that police officers are able to do this – because only by accepting our own flaws can we improve. When answering this question, try and consider the following:

- What was the situation, and who was giving you feedback?

- What was the feedback? Was it positive or negative?

- How did you respond to this feedback?

- How did you use this feedback to improve your working practice?

Write your answer in the textbox below, and then compare it to our response!

Sample Response

"I am someone who is able to take criticism extremely well, and always do my best to handle it in as constructive a manner as possible. I believe this is something that originally resulted from my university degree, where I was subjected to large amounts of criticism and honest feedback. As a result, I have developed thick skin, and am now able to use constructive feedback to my advantage.

A good example of this was during my previous position as a History teacher. One of my lessons was observed by my head of department. This was a yearly observation, which was conducted during regular lesson time, with the aim of assessing the continuous quality of members of staff at the school.

Although I felt that the lesson went really well, my head of department had a few things to give feedback on, that she felt I could improve. I was surprised by this, but I took her feedback with an open mind and fully accepted the comments.

Her primary concern was that I was perhaps pushing the students in my class a little too hard. As she correctly pointed out, we were not due to cover the area of the curriculum that I had been teaching for another week. Feeling that my class were up to the challenge, I had pushed ahead early for this. I agreed with her that I had overestimated the group, who were not quite ready for the new material. I have a tendency to be a little too enthusiastic with pushing the learning boundaries of my pupils. While this can pay off, and there are good intentions behind it, I accept that there is a time and a place for this.

Using the feedback provided, I made immediate changes to my next lesson, which had involved trying to incorporate the same approach. I was flexible enough to recognise that I had made a mistake and learned from the feedback from my head of department.

Although I am a highly-experienced professional, I am still capable of improvement and absolutely welcome the opportunity to do so."

Q14. Can you give me an example of a time when you have made improvements to your working practice, without the help of others?

How to Answer

As you know, **personal awareness** is a really important competency. It's vital that police officers are aware of their mood, and how it can impact their performance. More than this though, it's also important for officers to recognise when they've made mistakes, take ownership for these errors, and do their utmost to improve in the future. This question is essentially asking you to demonstrate a time when you've identified a personal mistake, and endeavoured to fix it. When answering this question, think about the following:

- What was the mistake that you made, and what were the consequences of you making it?

- What were the reasons for why this mistake occurred?

- How did you spot the error?

- What was your immediate reaction to the error?

- How did you go about resolving it?

Write your answer in the textbox below, and then compare it to our response!

Sample Response

"I work as a call handler for a large independent communications company. Part of my role involves answering a specific number of calls per hour. If I do not reach my target then this does not allow the company to meet its standards. After 6 months on the job, I found that I was falling behind on the number of calls answered. I was struggling to keep up, but I couldn't seem to work out why. In order to resolve this, I asked my manager to provide me with all of my past recorded calls. It then became apparent that I was taking too long speaking to the customers about issues that were irrelevant to the call itself. Because I am a conscientious and caring person I found myself asking the customer how they were and what kind of day they were having. Despite the customers being more than pleased with level of customer care, this approach was not helping the company and therefore I needed to change my approach.

I immediately went and spoke to my line manager, asking him whether it was possible for me to participate in extra call handling training, and further development courses. He was happy for me to do this. After the training, which took two weeks to complete, I was meeting my targets with ease. This in turn helped the company to reach its call handling targets."

Q15. Can you give me an example of when you have had to deal with setbacks, and how you overcame them?

How to Answer

This is another interesting question. Again, this question wants you to identify which competencies best fit under the bracket of 'dealing with setbacks'. In this case, the best fit would be **problem solving**, and then either **service delivery** or **teamworking** (depending on the situation that you answer with). Dealing with setbacks is an important part of working for the police. The nature of the job means that there will be times when things don't go the way you've planned, as there are many unpredictable elements when it comes to solving crime. Police Scotland want candidates who are resilient, hardworking and dedicated. They do not want candidates who will wilt under the slightest form of pressure, or give up after a setback. When answering this question, think about the following:

- What was the situation that you were dealing with at the time?

- What was the setback, or setbacks, and how did they occur? What was the reason for these?

- How did you respond to these setbacks?

- How did your resolution to these setbacks impact the final outcome of the task?

Write your answer in the textbox below, and then compare it to our response!

Sample Response

"After reading an appeal in my local paper from a local charity, I decided to try to raise money for this worthwhile cause by organising a charity car wash day at the local school during the summer holidays. I decided that the event would take place in a month's time, which would give me enough time to organise such an event. The head teacher at the school agreed to support me during the organisation of the event and provide me with the necessary resources required to make it a success.

I set about organising the event and soon realised that I had made a mistake in trying to arrange everything on my own, so I arranged for two of my work colleagues to assist me.

Once they had agreed to help me I started out by providing them with a brief of what I wanted them to do. I informed them that, in order for the event to be a success, we needed to act with integrity and professionalism at all times. I then asked one of them to organise the booking of the school and arrange local sponsorship in the form of buckets, sponges and car wash soap to use on the day, so that we did not have to use our own personal money to buy them. I asked the second person to arrange advertising in the local newspaper and radio stations so that we could let the local community know about our charity car wash event, which would in turn hopefully bring in more money on the day for the charity.

Following a successful advertising campaign, I was inundated with calls from local newspapers about our event and it was becoming hard work having to keep talking to them and explaining what the event was all about. But I knew that this information was important if we were to raise our target of £500.

Everything was going well right up to the morning of the event, when I realised we had not got the key to open the school gates. It was the summer holidays so the caretaker was not there to open the gates for us. Not wanting to let everyone down, I jumped in my car and made my way down to the caretaker's house and managed to wake him up and get the key just in time before the car wash event was due to start. In the end the day was a great success and we all managed to raise £600 for the local charity. Throughout the event I put in lots of extra effort in order to make it a great success.

Once the event was over I decided to ask the head teacher for feedback on how he thought I had managed the project. He provided me with some excellent feedback and some good pointers for how I might improve in the future when organising events. I took on-board his feedback in order to improve my skills."

Q16. Give me an example of a time when you have had to make a decision, that was in conflict with the views of the other members of your team.

How to Answer

This question is again assessing your leadership qualities, but in a different way to before. Now, the assessors want you to demonstrate that you have the capability of standing by your decisions when you know that they are right. This is an extremely important quality to have. Yes, it's great to consider the views of others, but if you know that you are right then you shouldn't back down, and you should be able to take ownership and responsibility for your judgement calls. As mentioned, part of working as a police officer means that you are a resilient person, who is confident in your own ability. There's a fine line between resilience and stubbornness, and this question wants you to address that. When answering this question, think about the following:

- What was the situation?

- At the time of the situation, what was your role in the team?

- What did the other members of your team want to do about the situation? Why did they have a conflicting view to you?

- What made you stand by your decision, and what did you do to enforce this?

- What was the outcome of this?

Write your answer in the textbox below, and then compare it to our response!

Sample Response

"Whilst working in my current position as a sales person, I was the duty manager for the day, as my manager had gone sick. It was the week before Christmas and the shop was very busy.

During the day the fire alarm went off, and I started to ask everybody to evacuate the shop, which is our company policy. The alarm has gone off in the past but the normal manager usually lets people stay in the shop whilst he finds out if it's a false alarm.

This was a difficult situation because the shop was very busy, nobody wanted to leave and my shop assistants were disagreeing with me in my decision to evacuate the shop. Some of the customers were becoming irate as they were in the changing rooms at the time. The customers were saying that it was appalling that they had to evacuate the shop and that they would complain to the head office about it. The sales staff were trying to persuade me to keep everybody inside the shop, and saying that it was most probably a false alarm as usual. I was determined to evacuate everybody from the shop for safety reasons, and would not allow anybody to deter me from my aim. The safety of my staff and customers was at the forefront of my mind, even though it wasn't at theirs.

Whilst remaining calm and in control, I shouted at the top of my voice that everybody was to leave, even though the sound of the alarm was reducing the impact of my voice. I then had to instruct my staff to walk around the shop and tell everybody to leave whilst we investigated the problem. I had to inform one member of staff that disciplinary action would be taken against him if he did not co-operate. Eventually, after I kept persisting, everybody began to leave the shop. I then went outside with my members of staff, took a roll call and awaited the Fire Brigade to arrive.

At first I felt a little apprehensive and under pressure, but was determined not to move from my position, as I knew 100% that it was the right one. I was disappointed that my staff did not initially help me, but the more I persisted the more confident I became. Eventually the Fire Brigade showed up, and they discovered that there was in fact a small fire at the back of the store. Luckily nobody was harmed, but the consequences could have been severe if I hadn't got everyone out.

This was the first time I had been the manager of the shop so I felt that this situation tested my courage and determination. By remaining calm I was able to deal with the situation far more effectively. I now felt that I had the courage to manage the shop better and had proven to myself that I was capable of dealing with difficult situations. I had learnt that staying calm under pressure improves your chances of a successful outcome dramatically."

Q17. Can you give me an example of a time when you have had to work with someone you weren't familiar with, to resolve a problem?

How to Answer

It's really important to understand that, as a police officer, you won't just be working in tandem with your colleagues. If you are the type of person who is uncomfortable working with people, then this is going to be a difficult role for you, because police officers need to be able to communicate with and work alongside members of the public. You need to be a reassuring and friendly presence, who is capable of responding to the needs of different members of the community. Therefore, your ability to work with people who you aren't familiar with is crucial. When answering this question, think about the following:

• What was the situation?

• Who were the (unfamiliar) individuals that you needed to work with? How did you go about establishing a rapport?

• What difficulties did you face in working with these people, and how did you overcome this?

• What was the end result?

Write your answer in the textbox below, and then compare it to our response!

Sample Response

"Whilst driving along the motorway I noticed that an accident had just occurred up in front of me. Two cars were involved in the accident and some people in the car appeared to be injured. There were a number of people stood around looking at the crash and I was concerned that help had not been called. We needed to work as a team to call the emergency services, look after the injured people in the cars and try to stay as safe as possible.

I became involved through pure instinct. I'm not the type of person to sit in the background and let others resolve situations. I prefer to try to help out where I can and I believed that, in this situation, something needed to be done. It was apparent that people were hurt and the emergency services had not been called yet. There were plenty of people around but they weren't working as a team to get the essentials done.

I immediately shouted out loud and asked if anybody was a trained first aid person, nurse or doctor. A man came running over and told me that he worked for the British Red Cross and that he had a first aid kit in his car. He told me that he would look after the injured people but that he would need an assistant. I asked a lady if she would help him and she said that she would. I then decided that I needed to call the emergency services and went to use my mobile phone.

At this point a man pointed out to me that if I used the orange emergency phone it would get through quicker and the operator would be able to locate exactly where the accident was. I asked him if he would call the emergency services on the orange phone, as he appeared to know exactly what he was doing. I noticed a lady sat on the embankment next to the hard shoulder crying and she appeared to be a bit shocked.

I asked an onlooker if he would mind sitting with her and talking to her until the ambulance got there. I thought this was important so that she felt supported and not alone. Once that was done, the remaining onlookers and I decided to work as a team to remove the debris lying in the road, which would hinder the route for the oncoming emergency service vehicles.

I decided to take the initiative and get everyone working as a team. I asked the people to let me know what their particular strengths were. One person was first aid trained and so he had the task of attending to the injured. Everyone agreed that we needed to work together as a team in order to achieve the task.

I took control of a deteriorating situation and got everybody who was stood around doing nothing involved. I made sure I asked if anybody was skilled in certain areas such as first aid and used the people who had experience, such as the man who knew about the orange emergency telephones. I also kept talking to everybody and asking them if they were OK and happy with what they were doing. I tried my best to co-ordinate the people with jobs that I felt needed to be done as a priority.

The benefit overall was for the injured people, ensuring that they received treatment as soon as possible. However, I did feel a sense of achievement that the team had worked well together even though we had never met each other before. I also learnt a tremendous amount from the experience.

At the end we all shook hands and talked briefly and there was a common sense of achievement amongst everybody that we had done something positive. Without each other we wouldn't have been able to get the job done."

Q18. **Can you give an example of when you have utilised your communication skills, to deliver bad news?**

How to Answer

Unfortunately, being a police officer means that there are times when you'll be required to break bad news to members of the public. This can be emotionally taxing, and is one of the hardest parts of the role. It will constitute a huge test of your communication skills, and you will need to be extremely sensitive and professional when placed in this position. Police officers must be capable of communicating with everyone however, and therefore it's integral that you can behave in an appropriate manner. When answering this question, try and consider the following:

- What was the nature of the news that you were delivering? Who were you delivering it to?

- What did you need to take into account, before breaking the news?

- How did you go about breaking the news, in a sensitive fashion?

- What steps did you take to try and comfort those involved?

- Did you arrange any follow up measures, after the incident?

Write your answer in the textbox below, and then compare it to our response!

Sample Response

"Sadly, yes, this was something I had to deal with last year. The people involved were my elderly next-door neighbours. They had a cat that they had looked after for years and they were very fond of it. I had to inform them that their cat had just been run over by a car in the road. I was fully aware of how much they loved their cat and I could understand that the message I was about to tell them would have been deeply distressing. They had cherished the cat for years and to suddenly lose it would have been a great shock to them.

To begin with I knocked at their door and ask calmly if I could come in to speak to them. Before I broke the news to them I made them a cup of tea and sat them down in a quiet room away from any distractions. I then carefully and sensitively told them that their cat had passed away following an accident in the road. At all times I took into account their feelings and I made sure I delivered the message sensitively and in a caring manner.

I took into account where and when I was going to deliver the message. It was important to tell them in a quiet room away from any distractions so that they could grieve in peace. I also took into account the tone in which I delivered the message and I also made sure that I was sensitive to their feelings. I also made sure that I would be available to support them after I had broken the news. The next day, following the incident, I went round to check on the couple and see how they were feeling. Whilst they were still extremely sad, they informed me that they were grateful for the way I had treated them, and that I had been so sensitive to the issue."

Q19. Can you give me an example of a time when you have implemented a positive change in the workplace?

How to Answer

Police Scotland want their employees to take a proactive approach to improvement. This doesn't only have to be for self-improvement, but for the whole workforce too. They want candidates who can inspire those around them to be better, and who can find solutions and improvements for the whole workforce. This question directly challenges your ability to do that, and your ability to spot improvements and amendments that could be made to general working practice. Try not to just talk about an improvement that you made to your own work. Try to find an example of where you've suggested a positive change, which helped everyone. When answering this question, consider the following:

- How did you notice that a change needed to be made?

- What was the problem, and how did you go about addressing it?

- Did you gain the views/opinions of your colleagues before tackling this?

- Was there a positive outcome, as a result of your intervention?

- Did this have a wider impact on the company as a whole?

Write your answer in the textbox below, and then compare it to our response!

Sample Response

"In my previous employment as a customer services assistant I was required to work closely with the general public on many occasions. Often, I would be required to provide varied solutions to customers' problems or complaints after listening to their concerns. It was always important for me to listen carefully to what they had to say and respond in a manner that was both respectful and understanding.

On some occasions I would have to communicate with members of the public from a different race or background and I made sure I paid particular attention to making sure they understood how I was going to resolve their problems. I would always be sensitive to how they may have been feeling on the other end of the telephone.

Every Monday morning the team that I was a part of would hold a meeting to discuss ways in which we could improve our service to the customer. During these meetings I would always ensure that I contributed and shared any relevant experiences I had during the previous week. Sometimes during the group discussions, I would find that some members of the group were shy and not very confident at coming forward, so I always sensitively tried to involve them wherever possible.

I remember on one occasion during a meeting I provided a solution to a problem that had been on-going for some time. I had noticed that customers would often call back to see if their complaint had been resolved, which was often time-consuming for the company to deal with. So, I suggested that we should have a system where customers were called back after 48 hours with an update of progress in relation to their complaint. My suggestion was taken forward and is now an integral part of the company's procedures. I found it quite hard at first to persuade managers to take on my idea, but I was confident that the change would provide a better service to the public we were serving."

Q20. Teamwork is a very important part of working within Police Scotland. However, police officers also need to be able to work independently and unsupervised. Could you provide me with an example of when you've done this in the past?

How to Answer

As the question states, while Police Scotland highly value teamwork, it's also essential that officers can work independently and unsupervised. You will always have the support of your colleagues, but there are times when you'll need to work on your own. Therefore, it's important for Police Scotland to establish that you are capable of this. When answering this question, think about the following:

- What was the situation?

- Why did the circumstances require you to work independently?

- Were there any particular methods that you used, to ensure that you worked effectively?

- Did you need to overcome any obstacles?

- What was the end result of the task?

Write your answer in the textbox below, and then compare it to our response!

Sample Response

"Yes, I have worked on my own unsupervised on numerous occasions. Most recently I was asked by the foreman on a building site to install new gas boilers in four properties within a tight deadline. Whilst I understood it was important to carry out the task quickly, there was no way I was going to compromise on safety. I started off by creating a mini action-plan in my head which detailed how I would achieve the task. I set about installing the first boiler conscientiously and carefully whilst referring to the safety manual when required. I made sure that there was sufficient ventilation in the houses as required under health and safety law.

During the week that I was required to complete the task I had previously arranged to go to a birthday party with my wife, but I decided to cancel our attendance at the event as I needed to get a good night's sleep after each hard day's work. I knew that if I was to maintain the concentration levels required to work safely and achieve the task then I would need to be in tip-top condition and getting sufficient rest in the evenings was an important part of this. By the end of the fourth day I had successfully completed the task that was set by the foreman and the proceeding safety checks carried out by the inspector on the boilers proved that I had done a very good job."

Q21. Can you give me an example of a time when you have worked with a colleague, to help improve their performance?

How to Answer

This question is again asking you to demonstrate the core competency of **teamwork**. It's important that police officers can work constructively together, to achieve organisational goals. Part of being a good co-worker is helping your colleagues when possible, to improve their own methods, and become more valuable members of the police service. When answering this question, think about the following:

- What was the situation? Did you approach your colleague, or did they approach you?

- What steps did you take to help them improve?

- Did you need to overcome any obstacles, or change your initial plan?

- How did your colleague respond to your help?

- What was the outcome?

Write your answer in the textbox below, and then compare it to our response!

Sample Response

"Prior to applying for this role, I worked as a teacher. During my last position, I was required to work with a teaching assistant who was fairly new to the role. She had just finished her training and was conducting a period of assistance in the classroom, before she would aim to go on and become a teacher herself.

On the first day that the assistant entered my classroom, she was extremely nervous, and actually seemed scared of the students. I noticed this straight away, took her to one side and assured her that I had complete confidence in her ability, and that she could come to me if she needed any help. I explained what I would require her to do during the lesson and gave her some brief pointers on how to go about doing these. I made sure to confirm that she was 100% happy and clear with this before we started teaching.

As the lesson progressed, I went around the room working with different groups of students. I asked the teaching assistant to do the same, and at some points we met in the middle and conducted in-depth discussion with the students together. I was really impressed by the depth of her knowledge, but did notice one or two pointers which I could give feedback on. At all times, I made sure to encourage the assistant and engage with her on a subject level. I felt it was important to increase her confidence and show her that she was truly capable of being a great teacher.

At the end of the lesson, I sat down with the assistant to give her some feedback. I made sure that I provided her with lots of praise for the level of subject knowledge she had displayed and the way she had integrated herself with the class, despite being nervous beforehand. I gave her some pointers on communication and getting her ideas across to the students. Overall, I made sure that she felt good about her own performance and happy that she was on the right track.

I am pleased to say that after a few months of working together, the assistant went on to complete her integration into teaching and became a fantastic teacher, in a nearby school."

Q22. Can you give me an example of a time when you have put the needs of the team before yourself?

This is an interesting question, because while it doesn't directly ask you about your teamworking skills, it does assess you on a key area of **teamwork** – which is being able to recognise the needs of the collective, and placing this above your own preferences. In your answer, you should give an account which demonstrates your understanding of why the team's goal is more important than your own goal, and your ability to prioritise what would be better for the collective than just for you. When answering this question, think about the following:

- What was the situation, and why did it require you to place the team's needs above your own?

- What were your individual preferences, and why did these contrast with those of the team?

- How did your behaviour help to resolve the issue for the team?

- What was the end result of the situation?

Write your answer in the textbox below, and then compare it to our response!

Sample Response

I like to keep fit and healthy and in order to do so, I play football for a local Sunday team. I am the captain of the team, and therefore it is my job to lead both on and off-the pitch.

In our last season, we had worked very hard to get to the cup final and were playing a very good opposition team who had recently won the league title. The team consisted of 11 players who regularly spend time together during training sessions and at social events. After only ten minutes of play, one of our players was sent off and we conceded a penalty as a result. One goal down, with 80 minutes left to play, we were faced with a mountain to climb.

However, we all remembered our training and worked very hard in order to prevent any more goals being scored. Due to playing with ten players, I immediately decided that I had to switch positions and play as a defender, something that I am not used to. I usually play as a striker, and therefore it was extremely difficult for me to adapt and move to the other end of the pitch. In the past, I have had very negative experiences of playing as a defender, and therefore this was something that I really didn't want to do. However, as captain I felt my role was to encourage the other players to keep going and to not give up until the final whistle had sounded. So, I moved positions. All the other players supported each other tremendously and the support of the crowd really pushed us on. The team worked brilliantly to hold off any further opposing goals and after 60 minutes we managed to get an equaliser. The game went to penalties in the end and we managed to win the cup.

Three days after the cup final, I contacted the other members of the team in order to organise a meeting. While we had celebrated on the night, I was determined not to let us rest on our laurels. Winning the cup was a fantastic achievement, but the only way that we could repeat this the following year would be with hard work. I was also determined for us to win the league, which we had underperformed in. In order to help me do this, I got into contact with someone who had recorded the whole match. After the individual in question generously sent me the files free of charge, I sat down at my laptop and watched the entire 90-minute game back. Whilst I did this, I took detailed notes in relation to each player and how I felt they could improve/ what they did well. I placed all of these notes onto a USB stick.

On the day of the meeting, the whole team sat down and we went through what I had observed from the tape. While they were surprised at the level of detail I had gone too, my teammates were extremely grateful for my input, and took my advice on board. I sent them the USB notes, and we began to work on each individual's strengths/weaknesses in training. The following year, we won the league and retained the cup. I believe that this was down to our team unity, and my man management techniques.

Overall, I believe that I am an excellent team player, and I will always put the needs of the team above my own. I understand that being an effective team member is very important if Police Scotland is to provide a high level of service to the community that it serves."

Q23. Can you give an example of when you have strengthened the relationship between individuals or a group of people?

How to Answer

This question is essentially asking you to demonstrate that you have the **communication skills** needed to work within Police Scotland. However, what's really important about this question is the way that it's worded. The question wants you to show that you can use your communication skills to make a genuine difference, and bring people together, who might otherwise misunderstand one another or don't get along. Whether it's developing relationships with your colleagues, or dealing with members of the public, it's very important that you can build bridges between different groups of people and that can everyone associated with Police Scotland can work in an amicable fashion. When answering this question, think about the following:

- What were the issues that needed to be overcome?

- What did you consider when dealing with the individuals or group?

- What was the outcome?

- How did you feel about dealing with the situation in the way that you did?

Write your answer in the textbox below, and then compare it to our response!

Sample Response

"Whilst working in a large warehouse as a factory worker, I was acutely aware of tensions between different workers. These tensions had been ongoing for a number of years. I believed the tensions centred on a breakdown in communication between different groups of people who worked at the warehouse.

In particular, there were tensions between white male workers and Asian male workers. I decided that something needed to be done, and so set about speaking to people within the different groups, to see what the issues were and whether there was any desire within the groups to break down these barriers once and for all. After speaking to key members of each group of workers, I came to the conclusion that the main reason for the barriers was simply down to a lack of understanding and respect.

In order to improve relations between the groups, I asked my manager for permission to hold a teambuilding day. I explained to him the benefits of investing time and money into breaking down the barriers between the groups of men, and he wholeheartedly agreed that it was a positive idea. I was aware of a company, situated not too far from the factory, that ran these types of days. I then arranged a date for the teambuilding day to take place and informed all members of staff of the event and how they could take part.

The teambuilding day would consist of different group events that were designed to build morale, improve communications and encourage team spirit. On the day of the event I had pre-arranged for people from the two groups to be on different teams, so as to encourage them to start mixing with each other and communicating more effectively. As soon as the first event started I sensed an improvement in relations and communication between the men.

This was immensely satisfying to see. Once the teambuilding day was over I had arranged for everyone to attend a local restaurant, where they would all sit down together and socialise in a relaxed manner in order to continue the good work which had taken place during the day.

Everyone agreed that the teambuilding day had been a great success and the following day at work the atmosphere had improved considerably. A few weeks later my manager called me into his office to congratulate me on the event. He informed me that productivity within the factory had increased by 20%, and he attributed the increase to my efforts in breaking down the barriers between the factory workers."

Q24. Can you give me an example of a time when you have utilised your job knowledge, to resolve a difficult situation?

How to Answer

As you will be aware, job knowledge is a really important part of working as a police officer. The better you understand the core requirements of your role, and how they fit into Police Scotland's wider objectives, the better you will be able to act as an exemplary representative of the police service. Police Scotland don't just want a candidate who goes through the motions with their job, they are looking for someone who is enthusiastic and committed, who has made a conscious effort to understand every single element of the role. When answering this question, think about the following:

- What was the situation? What needed to be resolved?

- What have been the consequences if you had not intervened?

- What did you say/do? How did you utilise your job knowledge?

- What was the end result of this?

Write your answer in the textbox below, and then compare it to our response!

Sample Response

"Prior to applying for this role, I was working at a printing company, based in the South of England. My role was to ensure that the manufacturing process went smoothly, and I was second in command on the factory floor.

On the day in question, we had to deal with an extremely large order. This meant that there would be a major backlog on printing, and certain orders would be delayed. This meant that some of the staff were very stressed and having to work harder than they normally would in order to meet the deadlines. On top of this, the air conditioning in the factory had broken, meaning that the environment was extremely hot and uncomfortable.

Towards the end of the day, as I walked across the factory floor, I noticed that two of my colleagues were arguing. The argument was very heated, and they were both becoming more and more angry. It seems that the disagreement resulted over the correct use of one of the printers in the factory. One of my colleagues felt that we should place extra paper into this printer, to maximise our output, whereas my other colleague wanted to use a different printer. Based on my experience, I realised that the first colleague was in fact right, and that we should have been doing it his way.

I quickly intervened in the argument and asked both individuals to calm down. I assured them that I totally understood their frustration with the situation, and that the company were hugely grateful for the hard work they were both putting in. I asked them whether they would prefer to discuss this issue in a quiet location. They both declined to do this.

Following this, I explained that the best way for us to proceed with printing would be to use colleague 1's suggestion. I proceed to tell both colleagues about exactly why this would be the best solution, and the advantages of using this compared to the other method. I also reassured colleague 2 that this was an easy mistake to make, and that he shouldn't feel bad about suggesting this. Both colleagues seemed satisfied with this, and got back to work.

I feel that my intervention helped hugely here. I resolved a potential conflict within the workplace environment, using my job knowledge, and dealt with my colleagues in a sensitive and courteous manner."

Q25. Have you ever dealt with a bullying incident at work? How did you respond to this?

How to Answer

Just as with any organisation, Police Scotland take a zero-tolerance stance on bullying or any associated behaviour. Although this isn't a listed core competency, it falls under the category of **respect for diversity** and **job knowledge**. It's extremely important that you are someone who can challenge unacceptable behaviour. Respect for diversity means that you can take an open and respectful approach to people from all different types of background, and that you treat every single person you meet with the utmost professionalism and fairness. When answering this question, think about the following:

- What was the situation? How did you become aware of the bullying/ unacceptable behaviour?

- What was your immediate reaction to this?

- How did you follow up on the incident? Did you take it to someone senior, or did you intervene directly yourself?

- What was the end result of your intervention?

Write your answer in the textbox below, and then compare it to our response!

Sample Response

"My personal policy on bullying is of absolutely no-tolerance, and I would fully expect any organisation that I am working at to take the same attitude. The workplace environment should be a place where people feel safe.

Whilst working in my previous role, as a teacher, I had to deal with at least one bullying incident. One of these incidents occurred between three of the students in my form group. The bullying first came to my attention when I witnessed one of the students crying outside of the classroom. After comforting and questioning the individual, who wouldn't tell me what the problem was, I resolved to keep a close eye on the situation in the future. I didn't have to wait long, as the very next day I witnessed a scene outside of the school gates where two students from my form group appeared to be teasing and picking on the aforementioned pupil, who seemed very upset. I witnessed this again during form time, and decided to take action.

I asked the student who was upset to stay behind at the end, and quizzed him on the nature of the interaction. He confessed that the other two pupils had been teasing him for a long time now, and at times had become physically aggressive with him. He had asked them to stop, but they had refused, and he had started to dread coming to school.

Realising that I was dealing with a bullying incident, I immediately took a statement from the student and asked him if he would be happy to come with me to student services. I assured him that he wasn't in any trouble, and that I would do everything possible to resolve the situation for him and prevent this from happening again. I made sure I comforted the student and made it clear that this kind of behaviour would not be tolerated. Once we arrived at student services, I sat with the student as they took a statement from him. We then interviewed the two pupils who had been bullying him, who at first denied culpability, but soon admitted to their behaviour. Together with student services, we firmly demonstrated to the two students that their behaviour was wrong and their parents were called. The two boys were suspended.

Student services thanked me for my actions, and asked me to keep a close eye on the student who had been the victim of such unacceptable behaviour. I feel that my observation and resultant action played a key role in resolving this situation, and ensuring that the pupil in question could come to school unafraid and feel respected by those within the school. Bullying of any kind should not be tolerated."

Motivations and
Values Questions

Now that we've covered the competency-based questions, let's move onto a different form of question, which you might be more familiar with. Motivations and values questions are commonplace in any form of interview. They are essentially questions which are formed around getting to know you as a person, to work out whether you are the right fit for the organisation. It's very important for the police to establish that you are applying for the right reasons. They don't want candidates who are applying 'to ride around in a police car with flashing lights'. They want candidates who are applying because they share the same values as the police – candidates who want to make a genuine difference in the community and protect the general public. So, you can expect questions such as:

'Tell me about why you are applying for this role.'

'What do you know about Police Scotland?'

'How do you think you can cope with the demands of the job?'

The motivations and values questions are likely to test you heavily on how well you've researched the job position. The police need to know that you understand what you are getting into, and won't quit as soon as the going gets tough. They also want to see that you have a genuine interest in their organisation. Conducting substantial research before application will show the police that you are serious about the role, and enthusiastic about the prospect of working for them.

Now, let's get started with some motivations and values questions. Just like before, we've given you a full response to every single one.

Q1. Tell us about why you want to become a police officer.

How to Answer

This is an incredibly common opening question, and it would be a huge surprise if you didn't hear this during your interview. The best response here, is to be honest! Think about the reasons for why you want to become a police officer. What has motivated you to apply? What is it about the police service that inspires you? Take a look at the goals and aims of Police Scotland on their website. Do you share these goals?

Write your answer in the textbox below, and then compare it to our response!

Sample Response

"I have wanted to become a police officer for almost four years now, and I can distinctly remember the time I decided this would be the job for me. I was walking through my local high street on my way to the gym on an early Saturday morning, when I noticed two police officers dealing with an aggressive and verbally abusive young man who, from what I understood later on, had been caught shoplifting from the newsagents in the high street. Whilst walking past, I stopped a few yards on, to see how the police officers would handle the situation.

The two police officers remained totally calm and in control of the situation, despite the abuse being directed at them by the man. Their body language was non-confrontational, and they appeared to be using well-thought out techniques to get him to calm down. Once the man had calmed down, the officers arrested him and took him away in their police car. From that point on I wanted to learn more about the role of a police officer. I felt that, due to my previous experiences in the Armed Forces and also my natural abilities, I had what it takes to become a competent police officer. I studied your website and also learnt all about the core competencies of the role. I then realised that I had the potential to become a police officer, and I have been waiting to apply ever since. In addition to this, I have lived in the local community for virtually all my life, and I feel proud that we live in a society that is, overall, safe and a great place to live. I understand a large part of the role of being a police officer is reactive, but I would also be interested in working on the proactive and educational side of the job, whereby you get to educate the public to help keep them safe and also prevent crime from happening in the first place.

Finally, whilst I very much like my current job, and feel a debt of gratitude to my employer, I am very much ready for a new challenge and the next stage of my career. I believe I would be an excellent police officer if successful, and can assure you I would work hard to uphold the principles and the values the force expects from its employees."

Q2. Tell me about yourself and what qualities you believe you have, that will be relevant to the role of a police officer.

How to Answer

This is another very common question. Remember, the purpose of this interview is to help Police Scotland find out more about who you are, and why you would be a great police officer. So, it's not unusual for them to just ask you this outright! Once again, your best response is to be honest in this situation. Think about what makes you a good fit for the role? What are your best qualities? How would they be of use to Police Scotland?

A word of caution when answering this, read the question! It's pretty easy here to go off on a tangent and reel off a big list of qualities that actually have nothing to do with the police service. Remember, you need to keep it relevant, and link your qualities back to what the police are looking for.

Write your answer in the textbox below, and then compare it to our response!

Sample Response

"To begin with, I am a hard-working, committed and highly-motivated person who prides himself on the ability to continually learn and develop new skills. I am 31 years old, and I currently work as a customer services manager for a transportation company. Prior to taking up this role approximately ten years ago, I spent five years working as a front-line soldier in the Army. In addition to being a family person, I also have my own hobbies and interests, which include team sports such as football and also playing the guitar in a local band.

I am a loyal person, who has a strong track record at work for being reliable, flexible and customer-focused. My annual appraisals are consistently to a high standard and I am always willing to learn new skills. Before applying for this job, I studied the role of a police officer and also the role of the police service in depth, to make sure I was

able to meet the requirements of the role. Having been working for my current employer for almost ten years now, I wanted to make sure that I had the potential to become a competent police officer before applying.

Job stability is important to me and my family. If successful, I plan to stay in the police force for many years.

Finally, I believe that the additional qualities I possess would benefit the role of a police officer. These include being physically and mentally fit, organisationally and politically aware, determined, reliable, an excellent team player, organised, committed, capable of acting as a positive role model for the police force and being fully open to change."

Q3. Tell me what work you have done during your preparation for applying to become a police officer.

How to Answer

As we mentioned during the introduction to this chapter, the police will want to know that you've conducted thorough preparation before applying. They want to see a level of dedication and enthusiasm right from the outset, and not just when you've got the job. Don't be surprised to encounter a question such as this, which directly challenges the amount of work you've put in beforehand. Remember too that there is enormous competition for jobs with Police Scotland. All of the other candidates (or the good ones anyway) will have put in strong amounts of preparation work beforehand – so you need to do your utmost to top this.

Write your answer in the textbox below, and then compare it to our response!

Sample Response

"I have carried out a huge amount of work, research and personal development prior to applying for this role. To begin with, I studied the role of a police officer, especially with regards to the core competencies. I wanted to make sure that I could meet the requirements of the role, so I asked myself whether I had sufficient evidence and experience to match each and every one of the core competencies.

Once I was certain that I had the experience in life, I started to find out more about the work the police carry out, both on a local and national level. I have studied your website in detail, and learnt as much as I possibly could about how you tackle crime, deal with the effects of it and also how you use statistics to drive down increasing crime trends in specific areas. I have also briefly read some of the important policing policies you employ. I wanted to make sure that I was prepared as possible for my interview today. In addition to reading and researching, I went along to my local police station to try and find out a bit more about the job, and the expectations that the public have from the police.

The police officer I spoke to was understandably very busy, but she did give me fifteen minutes of her time, whereby she explained what the job involved, what it was like working shifts and also the good points and challenging points about the job. After speaking with her, I felt I had a better understanding of the role and it only made me want to apply even more.

Finally, although I believe I am relatively fit, I started attending the gymnasium more to build up my physical strength and stamina. I also worked hard at increasing my times during the bleep test, and I can now get to level twelve since starting my application to join the police. I am very determined to become a police officer, and on that basis, I have carried out lots of research to find out as much as I could about the role."

Q4. The competition for this role is huge, but only a select few candidates will make it. Can you explain to me what you feel makes you better than the other applicants? Why should we hire you instead of them?

How to Answer

As we mentioned in the previous question, the competition for jobs with Police Scotland is incredibly fierce, so don't be surprised to hear a question such as this. They want to know what makes you better, and they won't be afraid to ask! The key to answering this question is to focus on your own positives, and what makes you a strong candidate. A bad response here will focus on the other candidates, and any perceived negatives. For example, if you start bad-mouthing the other applicants, then this will come across very badly to the interviewers. Focus on your own unique qualities, and how they will benefit the police!

Write your answer in the textbox below, and then compare it to our response!

Sample Response

"I believe I am the best candidate for this job for many reasons. First of all, I have been preparing for this role for many years now, by building up sufficient life experience and knowledge to be able to perform the role to a very high standard. Having studied all of the core competencies in detail, I feel I have plenty of experience to perform the duties of a police officer above and beyond the standards expected. I am a flexible person who will be available to work at all times, whether its day or night and also at weekends. I have a supportive family who fully understand, appreciate and support my dream of becoming a police officer with Police Scotland.

In addition to knowing my strengths, I am also aware of the areas I need to work on in order to improve, and I have been working on these to make sure I am fully prepared for the police training course, if successful. I have a good understanding and knowledge of the expectations that this police force expects from its staff, and I feel strongly that I will act as a good role model for the organisation that I am hoping to join.

Finally, I understand that we live in times where the police force is under more scrutiny than ever and the requirement to be an employee who is open to and supportive of change has never been greater. Once again, I feel strongly that I can adapt to a constantly changing environment, and provide the exceptional service that the public expects from its police officers. I can assure you that, if you give me the opportunity, I will not let you down and I will work harder than anyone to excel in the role."

Q5. Can you provide us with an example of a past work project that you successfully completed, and the obstacles you had to overcome?

How to Answer

Here you aren't being quizzed on the competencies, but on your core values and qualities. Your answer doesn't need to be as substantial in the previous section, but you still need to give the interviewers a high-quality response, which fully answers the question and showcases your ability.

Write your answer in the textbox below, and then compare it to our response!

Sample Response

"Yes, I can. I recently successfully completed a NEBOSH course (National Examination Board in Occupational Safety and Health) via distance learning. The course took two years to complete in total, and I had to carry out all studying in my own time, whilst holding down my current job as an Assistant Residential Building Site Manager.

I decided to fund and undertake this qualification myself in order to further develop my knowledge and skills of my role, and to also improve my ability to perform my job to a high standard. The biggest obstacle I had to overcome was finding the time to complete the work to the high standard that I wanted to achieve. I decided to manage my time effectively and allocated two-hours every evening of the working week in which to complete the work required. Initially, I found the time management difficult; however, I stuck with it and was determined to complete the course successfully. In the end, I achieved good results, and I very much enjoyed the experience and challenge. I also feel that I drastically improved my time management and organisational skills as a result of undertaking this course. I have a determined nature, and I have the ability to concentrate for long periods of time when required, whilst organising and undertaking multiple tasks concurrently. I can be relied upon to finish projects to a high standard."

Q6. What is your biggest strength?

How to Answer

We know, this is about as generic a question as possible, but it's one that you definitely need to practise answering! In almost any interview, you can expect to hear either this or 'what is your biggest weakness', so it's essential that you are prepared for it. When answering this question, be careful. The interviewer will want you to focus on one major strength. They don't want an entire speech on how great you are and all of your qualities. Focus on one major quality, and then elaborate on how you believe this can help the police.

Write your answer in the textbox below, and then compare it to our response!

Sample Response

"I believe that my biggest strength is in my ability to take leadership of difficult situations, and make crucial decisions. In my previous career, I have almost always worked in management positions, where I was required to make important decisions on a regular basis. I am well suited to dealing with large amounts of pressure and feel comfortable in making big decisions, as well as taking ownership and responsibility for these judgements.

I believe that this quality will strongly benefit me in my career as a police officer. I understand that working for the police involves large amounts of high-pressure decision making, and that officers must be able to remain calm and collected when the going gets tough. I feel that my decision-making skills would transfer over extremely well to the police, and that I would be able to benefit Police Scotland in this regard."

Q7. What is your biggest weakness?

How to Answer

Highly similar to the last question, this is another one which comes up in almost every single interview. If anything, this question is even more common than the previous, so you need to be prepared for it! When answering this question, try and focus on one weakness. However, pick a weakness which isn't too damaging. For example, if you tell the police that your biggest weakness is your underlying sympathy for criminals, then you are not going to get the job. Alternatively, if you tell the police that your biggest weakness is in your organisational skills – but that you are making a conscious effort to improve on this, then they will be far more likely to take you on.

Write your answer in the textbox below, and then compare it to our response!

Sample Response

"I would say that my biggest weakness is in my organisational skills. I do consider myself an organised person, but sometimes – especially when I have many projects on the go – I can tend to be a bit disorganised and get a little bit flustered. I'm working really hard to improve on this, as I understand that organisation is a very important quality for police officers to have. I believe that once I have learned how to improve my mindset, take a breath and just try to calm down, I can be extremely organised and deal with any number of tasks that I'm given."

Q8. Do you think the police force provide value for money to the public? If so, why?

How to Answer

During your interview, you can expect to be asked some questions based on areas such as public perception of the police, the police role in society, and your own perception of the police. When answering these types of questions, you should always try and be as positive as possible! It's very unlikely that the police are going to hire someone who comes into the interview with a negative perception about Police Scotland. They want to hire someone who is enthusiastic about the idea of performing police work, for a highly esteemed and respectable organisation – so be that person!

Write your answer in the textbox below, and then compare it to our response!

Sample Response

"Absolutely, I believe that the police force offers very good value for money. Whilst I very much want to become a police officer and work within the force, I too live in the local community and I have only seen great things from the police. From what I can see on a local level in my community, the police work very hard to educate the public and reduce crime, despite having limited resources. In fact, your website shows that the force is becoming more efficient in tackling crime than ever before. For example, your force has managed to reduce vehicle related crime by seventeen percent over the last twelve months. I was very impressed by those statistics. I would imagine that, whilst the media and press can be very helpful in helping the police to catch offenders and reduce crime, sometimes the police can be painted in a negative light by them. On that basis, I would imagine it would be part of my job as a police officer to act as a positive role model for the police. I would work hard to educate the public about the good work the force is doing, and demonstrate that value for money is being delivered."

Q9. You are attending a local school talking to the children about the work of the police force. The teacher asks you to explain to the children how to call 999 in an emergency. What would you tell them?

How to Answer

During the interview, it's highly likely that the assessors will try to put you on the spot, to test what kind of person you are. The above question is a perfect way of doing this, and your answer will tell the assessors a lot about you. For example, if you just give them a short answer, 'Push this button and speak to the operator' then they aren't going to get the best impression of you. Alternatively, if you talk the children through how to call the operator and explain exactly how and when this should be done, then the interviewers will gain a much more favourable view of you.

Write your answer in the textbox below, and then compare it to our response!

Sample Response

"Well firstly, I would tell them that they should only call 999 if it is an emergency. I would then give them examples of when to call 999, including if a crime is happening right now, someone is in immediate danger, there is a risk of serious damage to property, a suspect for a serious crime is nearby, or there is a traffic collision involving injury or danger to other road users. I would then use the opportunity to educate the children on why it is important they do not make hoax calls under any circumstances, as this could block the telephone lines for someone who really does need the police or other emergency services.

Following this, I would tell the children that the police do have an alternative number they can call if it is a non-emergency. The number they would need in a non-emergency situation is 101, and I would then give them additional examples of non-emergency situations, such as reporting a crime not currently in progress, giving information to the police about crime in their area, speaking to the police about a general enquiry and also contacting a specific police officer or member of staff. Finally, I would then ask the children if any of them had any questions, to make sure they understood the information I had provided them with."

Q10. **Can you give me an example of when you have challenged inappropriate behaviour?**

How to Answer

Like Question 5, here you will need to give the interviewers a personal example. Again, this doesn't need to be as comprehensive as the previous section, but you do need to demonstrate to the assessors that you have what it takes to challenge poor behaviour. You should still endeavour to give them a full run-through of the entire situation that occurred, what the behaviour was, and how you dealt with it. You need to give the assessors the best possible view of how your actions resolved the situation, and you can only do this by providing them with details. Remember that police officers would be expected to challenge any inappropriate behaviour that they see, both at the station and whilst out in public.

Write your answer in the textbox below, and then compare it to our response!

Sample Response

"Yes, I can. I currently work as an IT consultant and I was carrying out contract work for a large corporate company in Manchester. I was having a tea break on my own in the company canteen, when I overheard a man insulting one of his co-workers. The language that he used was incredibly offensive and unacceptable, and he was talking directly to her!

I immediately went over to the man and said in a calm and respectful manner that I found his comment to be offensive and requested that he didn't use that type of language, as it is unwelcome. I could sense he was angered by my comments, and he proceeded to tell me to mind my own business. I remained calm, and reiterated my request, by asking him once again not to use that type of offensive language in the workplace. I stated that, if he continued to use that type of language, I would report him to the company Managing Director.

He immediately changed his tone, apologised and then got up and left the canteen. I then spoke to the lady whom the comment was directed at and explained the reasons why I had intervened. She told me she was grateful for my interaction and said that he often spoke to her in that manner. To my amazement, she informed me that the man who made the comment was in fact her line manager. After I left the canteen, I sent an email directly to the Managing Director of the company informing her of what I had just witnessed in the canteen, whilst also explaining what I had done to prevent it from happening again.

I would never hesitate to challenge any type of behaviour that was either inappropriate, bullying in nature or discriminatory. This type of behaviour is not acceptable and should be challenged."

Q11. What type of work do you think you will be undertaking as a police officer, if you are successful?

How to Answer

This is another question which is designed to test your understanding of the role. As we've mentioned, the police are looking to take on candidates who fully understand what they are entering. If you tell the police that you don't know what type of work you'll be doing, then they will be unlikely to hire you. Police work is extremely hard, and they need candidates who are prepared for this, and willing to work hard to succeed. You don't need to provide the interviewer with an exact, in-depth job description, but they will expect you to have some knowledge of what jobs police officers need to do, what type of people they deal with, and what responsibilities they hold – as well as their role in society. This should be easy enough, provided you have researched beforehand.

Write your answer in the textbox below, and then compare it to our response!

Sample Response

"I believe the work I would undertake will be extremely diverse and varied in nature, and that the role would require me to use a wide remit of skills and expertise. To begin with, I would be acting as a positive role model for Police Scotland, by behaving with honesty and integrity; and delivering a service to the public that exceeds their expectations.

I would also be providing, on a daily basis, a reassuring high-visibility presence within the community, whilst also responding to incidents, gathering evidence and taking contemporaneous notes and statements of incidents and reports of crimes as and when they are reported. I would be required to attend and protect crime scenes, and also investigate incidents through effective policing and by also following my training and operational procedures at all times. I would make arrests when appropriate, complete custody procedures and also interview suspects and present evidence in court. I would liaise and work with other stakeholders and agencies, to make sure that we all worked towards the common goal of protecting the community in which we serve. I would also be required to put vulnerable people, victims of crime and witnesses first. I would be required to face challenging and difficult situations on a daily basis, and I would need to be at my best at all times to ensure I uphold the principles of policing. Finally, I would be required to adopt the core competencies of the police officer's role, and utilise interpersonal skills to diffuse and respond with integrity in any situation."

Q12. How can the police improve relations with Scottish communities?

How to Answer

This is a great question, but it's pretty tough to answer. Police Scotland are looking to hire individuals with an ability to spot solutions to problems, who can come up with innovative solutions, and think creatively. Remember that problem solving is one of the core competencies. Now, this doesn't mean that the interviewers are telling you right here and now to solve their problems, but asking this question puts you on the spot and lets them see how fast you can come up with solutions to problems. Your research should help here, and hopefully provide you with the backbones for a credible response. Remember to be positive about current police relations with the public, and the current effort that they are putting in!

Write your answer in the textbox below, and then compare it to our response!

Sample Response

"I think there are a number of different ways you can improve relations. I am sure you do many of these things already, but promoting all of the good work you do within the community, via the local press, will help to demonstrate to the public that the good work you are doing is making a difference to their lives. I also feel that working closely with community groups and community leaders can be a positive thing, to demonstrate that the police force is listening to people's concerns and issues.

I also think that it is very important that the police follow up and keep people updated with progress on policing matters. For example, if the police hold community meetings where local residents are encouraged to share their concerns, somebody must follow up with a progress report or communicate what work has been done to deal with their concerns, if they are a policing-related matter. I would also imagine that it is my responsibility as a police officer, if I am to be successful, to be as visible as possible within the community.

It would be my job to speak to people and reassure them that the police are there to serve them and provide a reassuring presence. I also feel that relations with the police has to start at an early age. I understand budgets must be very restricted, but if police officers are able to attend schools and talk to children from an early age about the type of work they do, that can only be a good thing and it will help to give the children a positive impression of the police from an early age.

Community policing, I would imagine, means working proactively and building relationships in the face of tension and issues. So, if there are problems within a particular area that I am serving, it would be my job to help ease those tensions and build better relationships with the community by working alongside community leaders. I guess the police service would cease to function without the active support of the communities it serves. Effective community engagement, targeted foot patrols and collaborative problem solving would significantly increase public confidence in policing activity."

Q13. Physical fitness is really important for Police Scotland. What do you do to keep yourself fit? Do you value fitness?

How to Answer

As the question states, it's extremely important that police officers are at peak physical fitness. A healthy body equals a healthy mind, and police officers are often required to take part in activities which will push them to their physical limitations – such as giving chase to criminals. Therefore, it's integral that you are a person who takes their physical fitness seriously. Along with this, it could be argued that keeping yourself in shape demonstrates a level of confidence and self-respect, which are both important qualities for a police officer to have.

Write your answer in the textbox below, and then compare it to our response!

Sample Response

"I take personal responsibility for my fitness and I fully understand how important this would be to my role as a police officer. At present, I go running four times a week in the mornings before I start work. I like to get up early and get my fitness routine out of the way, which then leaves me time to spend with my family once I get home from work.

I usually run five kilometres each time, and this ensures my body fat is kept to a healthy level and my concentration levels are at their peak. My current job involves me having to concentrate for long periods of time and I have a responsibility to make sure I can perform at work to a high standard. At weekends, I spend time playing hockey for a local team. We are not overly competitive; however, I like the fact I get to play a team sport and interact with other people from the community. We also go out together socially once a month and I really enjoy that side of being part of a hockey team."

Q14. Why do you think the police force is keen to recruit more people from black and ethnic minority groups, and do you have any suggestions for how we might achieve that aim?

How to Answer

As we mentioned, this interview will contain lots of questions based around popular topics within policing, and this is certainly a very popular topic of discussion. If you follow the news, you'll be aware that British police forces are making a sustained attempt to recruit individuals from minority backgrounds, so it's not unusual for you to be asked a question around this. Make sure you do your research beforehand, and you should have no problem with this one!

Write your answer in the textbox below, and then compare it to our response!

Sample Response

"If the police force is to deliver a consistently high level of service, then it needs to be representative of the community that it serves. Our community is diverse in nature, so the police service should reflect this if it is to achieve its aims and goals. The police could offer introductory programmes or courses to people who are looking to join the service from under-represented groups. These courses could aim to show people what it is like to work within the police service and also give them tours of police stations, the training centre and also give them the opportunity to speak to already serving police officers from black and ethnic minority backgrounds.

This type of introductory course or programme would give people the opportunity to learn more about the service, before they commit to applying. Conversely, it would also give the police the opportunity to find out why so few people from under-represented groups actually apply. This type of information might be invaluable to the police as there might be specific reasons why not enough people are joining.

I would imagine that many people consider applying to become a police officer but think it's not for them for a variety of reasons, such as not having the right levels of fitness or fear their decision won't be supported by family and friends. During this type of introductory course or programme, potential applicants could also take along with them their family and friends, which would in turn give them the support they need during their application to the police."

Q15. Can you tell me about a time when you have promoted and supported change in an organisation?

How to Answer

As you'll know from the competency section, it's extremely important that employees of Police Scotland can take an open mind to change and improvement, and that all members of the force play an equal role in implementing positive working changes. With this in mind, it should come as no surprise that the interviewers might ask you about when you've demonstrated this in the past. They are looking for candidates that have a positive attitude, who are always looking to improve, and therefore you need to be this person!

Write your answer in the textbox below, and then compare it to our response!

Sample Response

"I currently work as a care assistant for the Local Authority. Just a few months ago, all of the care workers were called into a meeting by the Area Manager. We all sat down in the meeting, and the Area Manager began to explain how a number of potentially disruptive changes to our working practices were coming into force very soon. The changes were required in order for our department to meet its care quality standards target. I could sense that a number of people within the room were unhappy with the suggestion of change, and they began to make their feelings known to the manager.

I put my hand up to speak, and made a suggestion to everyone in the room that we should give our manager the respect she deserves and allow her to at least finish explaining what the changes were, and how they would impact on our working lives, before voicing our own opinions.

Everyone then agreed to remain silent until the manager had finished her talk. The manager went on to explain that everyone would be affected within the department and, in particular, our shift patterns would alter, but that our total working hours would stay the same. She went on further to explain that we would all have the opportunity to work extra hours, at double-pay, if we wanted to. At the end of her talk, some of the care workers were still clearly upset and angered by the pending changes. After they had had the opportunity to express their feelings, I stated my own opinion to the group. I explained that we all work in an ever-changing environment, and we would all need to adapt to change, as the change would only increase as the years went on. I also explained that change could actually be a positive thing if we all embraced it, and at the very least, we should all give it a try.

Some people in the room seemed surprised at my positive attitude, and I think they expected me to be more "on their side", whilst they were challenging our Area Manager. One thing is for sure, I was not going to allow the negative talk some people were engaging in, to affect my own working life. At the end of the meeting, everyone agreed to at least try and embrace the changes. We also all agreed to meet up again in three months' time with our Area Manager, in order to discuss the changes and how we were getting on. I believe that my positive attitude and contributions during the meeting allowed the team to at least try to embrace the new changes that were coming into force."

Q16. What issues are affecting Police Scotland, as of the present day?

How to Answer

Again, this is a test of your pre-application research. If you've researched thoroughly beforehand, then you should have a good idea of how to answer this question. If not, then you'll flounder! You can focus your answer here either on the local community in which you'd be policing, or on Police Scotland as a whole – or better yet, both! Your explanation of the issues doesn't need to be in-depth, but it's important to acknowledge that you have looked into the force, and identified the areas which are critical for them to improve in. Of course, remember to be entirely complimentary about Police Scotland too!

Write your answer in the textbox below, and then compare it to our response!

Sample Response

"During my pre-application research, I was studying both the Police Scotland website and other useful online resources, to find out the types of issues impacting the police both locally and nationally. From what I understand, the police service is facing a number of challenges that will require highly effective leadership and the ability of police officers to adapt and change their working practices. For example, there has been a huge increase in cyber-related crime and incidents which need to be investigated. These, understandably, take up a huge amount of time and resources and can often be very difficult to investigate. In addition to cyber-related crime, the opportunities for people to actually report crime are far better than they used to be. Whilst this is very much a positive thing, collecting and using data and information relating to reported crimes and incidents can take time and resources. The police service has a huge challenge ahead of them in order to stay on top of reported crime and to also investigate incidents thoroughly.

I would also imagine there is a challenge for the police service in respect of which types of reported crime to prioritise, based on the limited resources it has at its disposal. Once again, police officers would need to be highly efficient in their work, to help the service achieve its goals and targets.

Another issue affecting the police service will be the recruitment of under-represented groups and BME officers. The police service needs to be representative of the communities in which it serves, if it is to continually provide the exceptional levels of service it currently provides. From my research and studies, I also understand there are challenges for the police service with regards to breaking the repeat offender cycle. Only by working with other agencies and stakeholders can the police service collate sufficient data and information to look at new ways to prevent people from reoffending. Whilst I am sure there are many other issues and challenges affecting the police service both locally and nationally, these were the ones that appeared prominent whist carrying out my research and studies."

Q17. Can you give an example of when you have supported diversity in the workplace?

How to Answer

As you'll know from the competencies section, respect for diversity is incredibly important. As a police officer you'll come into contact with a wide variety of people, from a diverse range of backgrounds, and therefore it's important that you can treat every person with the proper level of respect and fairness that they deserve. Naturally, the police want to know that you are someone who can do this before they employ you – as it would be a disaster for them to employ someone who didn't respect diversity. Remember that the police act as role models within society, and you must behave as an exemplary representative of Police Scotland if you are employed by them.

Write your answer in the textbox below, and then compare it to our response!

Sample Response

"I currently work as an office administrator for a small architect design business in London. We have an open plan office and there are 27 staff in total. It's a busy and friendly office, and we are always taking on new staff to cope with our expansion plans. Last month, a new member of the team joined. She was going to be working as an admin assistant, just like me, and I was keen to help her settle in and show her the ropes.

When she arrived, she came into the office in a wheelchair. I introduced myself to her straight away, made her feel welcome and said that I would show her to her new work station. As we made our way over to her desk, which was at the other end of the office, I suddenly realised that she would potentially have problems making her way to the toilets and also the kitchen area. Whilst our office building is equipped to accommodate people in wheelchairs, I felt the desk we had provided her with was not really in the best location.

I decided to make a suggestion to her. Basically, my desk is located not too far away from both the toilet facilities and also the kitchen area, and I told her that I was going to swap desks with her to make her life a bit easier in the office. She told me that I didn't need to do that, but I insisted. I told her that we were a very welcoming office and any other member of staff would also do the same. I then took the lady back over to my office space and started to move my things over to where her desk was located. It only took me twenty minutes to move all of my things to the new desk and I could sense the lady was pleased that I insisted on moving her to the better location. A few other members of the office team saw what I was doing, and they joined in by helping me move my things to the new desk.

This small act had a big impact on helping the new member of staff to settle in. Not only did she feel more valued and appreciated, but it also helped to make her recognise that we, as a company, support diversity and do all we can to ensure every member of staff feels welcome, valued and appreciated."

Q18. Working as a police officer can be very emotionally taxing. Do you think that you have what it takes to cope with this?

How to Answer

In this question, the assessor is directly questioning you on your ability to cope with some of the less-favourable elements about working for Police Scotland. As we have already explained, working as a police officer is not just physically difficult, but mentally too. In some ways, if you've never experienced it before, then you might have no idea about how you'd cope with breaking bad news to a family or relative of someone who has died or been injured – but this is something that you may have to do if you are working as a police officer, so you need to be prepared for it. In your answer, you should explain what you understand the assessor to mean by this statement, and try to reassure them that you do have what it takes.

Write your answer in the textbox below, and then compare it to our response!

Sample Response

"I fully understand that working as a police officer is difficult emotionally, and I am prepared to deal with this. I will be completely honest here, I have never been in a situation where I've had to break really bad news to someone, however I feel that I would be able to handle this responsibility. I consider myself to be someone who is emotionally resilient and very strong. I'm not easily upset by anything, and I am willing to take on the challenge. Furthermore, I understand that there is more to the emotional side of policing than just 'breaking bad news'. As an officer, I am aware that I will often be witness to things which would make an ordinary person uncomfortable, or upset them. In my personal life, I have had to deal with a number of emotional challenges, and I have always come through them with my head held high and my confidence intact. I fully believe that I could cope with the emotional demands of police work."

Q19. If a senior police officer told you to do something that you disagreed with, what would you do?

How to Answer

This is a really interesting question, and the answer should tell the assessors a great deal about your character. Have a think about the answer to this one, what would you actually do? What type of person would the police be looking for in this circumstance? How do you think they would want you to respond? Remember that discipline is extremely important within the police, and if your senior officer is asking you to do something, then there's probably a good reason for that!

Write your answer in the textbox below, and then compare it to our response!

Sample Response

"First and foremost, I would obey his or her orders, as long as it was a lawful order. I understand I am joining a disciplined service, and it would be important that I followed their instructions.

Then, if after the incident or situation there was an opportunity for me to express my view in a respectful, positive and constructive manner, I would do so. I would always respect instructions and orders given to me, and perform any task to the highest possible standard.

I fully understand the importance of following orders from senior officers, who are more qualified than me to make big decisions. I would always respect the decisions of a senior officer if employed by Police Scotland, provided those decisions are made within the confines of the law."

Q20. Can you explain to me why the core competencies are so important, and why it's vital for Police Scotland employees to follow these?

How to Answer

Hopefully the first section of this book has shown you how to answer this question! We've certainly already given you a full explanation for why the competencies are so important, so go back and study this before you write your response. This question ties into something which is very important for the police, which is the idea that it's not enough to just 'know' what the competencies or core behavioural expectations are, but you also need to understand why they are so important and how to use them.

Write your answer in the textbox below, and then compare it to our response!

Sample Response

"I understand that the core competencies are extremely important. In any organisation, it's essential to have a code of ethics and conduct that employees should measure their behaviour against, and this is even more important in the police. Police officers are role models within society. We have a duty to show the public about how they should behave, and hold ourselves to the highest possible standards. As an officer, I understand that I would be a representative of Police Scotland, its ethics and values. Not only would I be extremely grateful for the opportunity to represent the service, but I would do my utmost to uphold the outstanding reputation of the service. I am confident that I would be a fantastic member of your service, who could demonstrate the core competencies to their fullest."

Q21. What are the key priorities for this division?

How to Answer

This is a question that is more aimed at the division you are applying to, but it could also be expanded to include Police Scotland as a whole. Your research should give you a great idea of how to answer this. Think about the major issues that the force is dealing with, and the things they've already tried in order to tackle these.

Write your answer in the textbox below, and then compare it to our response!

Sample Response

"Having undertaken substantial research into this division and the local area, I already know the answer to this one. Your main priorities are as follows: dealing with anti-social behaviour, ensuring visible community policing is at the heart of everything you do, protecting the public from serious harm, providing a professional service by putting victims and witnesses first, meeting national commitments for policing, delivering value for money and also developing and supporting your workforce so they can do their job professionally and diligently.

One of the biggest reasons that I want to work for this division in particular, is that I found your goals and priorities were very close to my own, and thus I was hugely impressed. I am someone who believes wholeheartedly in safeguarding the community in which we live, and thus I found this division's priorities to be extremely admirable."

Q22. Tell me about which part of working for Police Scotland you think you'd like the most.

How to Answer

This is a nice and easy question, all you have to do is be honest in your answer. Obviously, give a sensible response. An answer such as, 'I would love driving around in the police car with flashing lights' will not impress the interviewer. Instead, focus on something that you know is important to the police force. For example, safeguarding the public.

Write your answer in the textbox below, and then compare it to our response!

Sample Response

"There's so many elements of working for the police that I think I'd enjoy, but the part I'd enjoy most is in having the opportunity to protect the people of the local community. I have lived in this area for my entire life, and I think it would be fantastic to give something back. Being employed as a police officer, and protecting the interests of the public, is the perfect way to do this. By working in tandem with my colleagues and everyone else at Police Scotland, I truly believe that we can make a difference – not just in this community but to Scotland as a whole."

Q23. What do you think will be the least enjoyable aspect of working for Police Scotland?

How to Answer

This is similar to the previous question, in that it should be fairly easy to answer, but you do need to be careful here. You should always aim to be positive about the police force, and it won't reflect well with the interviewers if you reel off a list of negatives before they've even employed you. You can be honest here, whilst still showing the interviewers that you are extremely excited and enthusiastic about the prospect of working for Police Scotland.

Write your answer in the textbox below, and then compare it to our response!

Sample Response

"While I'm hugely excited about the idea of working for Police Scotland, I understand that it's not an easy job, and there will of course be areas which I find difficult. I would say that the least enjoyable aspect, for me, will be in having to break bad news to people, or witnessing things which will be upsetting. While I'm an emotionally resilient person, and I can handle these things, they are probably the part about the job that I'm least looking forward to. That being said, I'm confident that this wouldn't be an issue, and I could excel at these areas – regardless of whether I enjoy them."

Q24. Have you discussed your application with your family? Do you have their support?

How to Answer

This might seem like a surprising question for the police to ask, but it's actually extremely important! Remember that working for the police is a really tough role. It won't just have an impact on you, but on your family too, and therefore it's very important for your family to be on board with your decision to join the police and with the type of work that you'll be doing. There are times when working as a police officer can be a dangerous role, as you will inevitably be placed in a position where you are required to deal with criminals. Likewise, the hours aren't always sociable, and this can take its toll. The police need to make sure that candidates' families are happy with their decision, because they don't want candidates who will quit later on due to family related concerns.

Write your answer in the textbox below, and then compare it to our response!

Sample Response

Yes, I have discussed my application to Police Scotland with my family, and I have their full support. Prior to application, I sat down with my family to discuss the full extent of my desire to join the police, and made them aware of both the risks, and the impact that this could have on our social life. Although I initially expected them to be reluctant, to my surprise they were really enthusiastic about me joining the police, and encouraged me to pursue this opportunity. My family has a good understanding of how much I admire Police Scotland, and that it's always been a dream of mine to join the service.

I am extremely grateful for their support, and determined to make them proud in this endeavour.

Q25. Do you have any questions for us?

How To Answer

The ending of an interview is really important, and this is a common question for you to hear. You need to leave the interviewers with a great impression of you, and what better way to do this than to follow up with some of your own questions? Before you attend the interview, it's always good to try and come in with at least 3 or 4 questions that you'd like to ask. This shows enthusiasm and interest in the police!

When asking your questions, just make sure that you are careful. You should avoid asking questions related to pay or holiday, and focus on topics such as the work you'll be doing, and the training they'll provide.

In the box below, write down some questions that you might have for the police.

WANT MORE HELP PASSING THE SCOTTISH POLICE SELECTION PROCESS?

CHECK OUT OUR OTHER TITLES:

FOR MORE INFORMATION ON OUR TESTING SERIES, PLEASE CHECK OUT THE FOLLOWING:

WWW.HOW2BECOME.COM